SCOREBOARD SOCCER

DAVID BAIRD

SCOREBOARD SOCCER

CREATING THE ENVIRONMENT TO DEVELOP YOUNG PLAYERS

Foreword by
KEVIN KEEGAN,
Two-Time Winner
of the Ballon d'Or

Meyer & Meyer Sport

British Library of Cataloguing in Publication Data
A catalogue record for this book is available from the British Library

Scoreboard Soccer
Maidenhead: Meyer & Meyer Sport (UK) Ltd., 2022
ISBN: 978-1-78255-232-1

© 2022 by Meyer & Meyer Sport (UK) Ltd.
Aachen, Auckland, Beirut, Dubai, Hägendorf, Hong Kong, Indianapolis, Cairo, Cape Town,
Manila, Maidenhead, New Delhi, Singapore, Sydney, Tehran, Vienna
🜲 Member of the World Sport Publishers' Association (WSPA), www.w-s-p-a.org

Credits
Cover and interior design: Isabella Frangenberg
Layout: DiTech Publishing Services, www.ditechpubs.com
Cover illustrations: Courtesy of David Baird
Bouncey Castle illustrations: Nat Jones
Interior diagrams: Courtesy of David Baird. All diagrams created by www.tacticalpad.com
Managing editor: Elizabeth Evans

Printed by: Print Consult GmbH, Munich, Germany
Printed in Slovakia

ISBN: 978-1-78255-232-1
E-Mail: info@m-m-sports.com
www.thesportspublisher.com

CONTENTS

FOREWORD

I have been fortunate enough to have had a long and successful career as a professional player, but I still consider my early days as a youth player among my fondest memories. A fun introduction to soccer with a coach who inspires and motivates their players to develop − not only as players, but as people − is invaluable.

When I met David in 2007 − when he was practically a youth himself − it was our shared passion for creating a fun environment in which to introduce young players to the game that brought us together. After hiring David as a coach, I witnessed his passion for providing children with opportunities to learn and play soccer. Fun was always at the forefront of his sessions, and those young players were desperate to come back, constantly asking for Coach David.

I am proud to see David has continued to develop his passion and, in writing this book, has shared his ideas with coaches worldwide. Furthermore, I am happy to endorse his terrific Scoreboard Soccer concept.

Not only does Scoreboard Soccer make sessions fun and inclusive, but it also provides a lot of opportunity for learning and individual feedback. David's method allows the coach to instill key values by praising skill, effort, and attitude through fun games. Praising such behaviors motivates players to repeat them, and, in time, positive habits such as bravery, creativity, and communication form.

When David explained his concept to me, I was impressed at how much it relates to the modern game, which is chaotic and ever changing. At any moment, players may be faced with a 3v2, 1v3, or 4v4, and they need to react and respond to these situations. Scoreboard Soccer not only gives players ample opportunity to learn through practical experience, but it also gives the coach a chance to highlight methods that will help players take advantage of these situations in future games.

During a Scoreboard Soccer session, players work incredibly hard, cover a lot of ground, and try their best to receive praise from the coach via the scoreboard. Essentially, David has created an environment that facilities physical, technical, and tactical development without the players even realizing it!

If, as a coach, you want to provide young players with a fun environment that presents challenges aligned with their individual playing experience and ability, then I highly recommend Scoreboard Soccer as a concept that will develop youth into the players – and people – you'll be proud of.

–Kevin Keegan

PREFACE

By 2015, twelve years into my time as a coach, I'd developed a strong admiration for the idea of letting the game be the teacher, particularly when working with young players.

During those twelve years, the players benefited greatly from a game-based approach to training, and the benefits heavily outweighed any drawbacks. But there were drawbacks. With my game-based approach, I wasn't sure if the players were being challenged; if they were being supported; if I were happy with the behavior being displayed by all players; if everyone was having fun; or if this were the most optimal learning environment that I could create.

After five years of constant "design, deliver, refine," I'm delighted to share with you the concept that transformed my previous answers to these questions into "Absolutely!"

I hope you and the players you work with enjoy *Scoreboard Soccer* and find the concept as fun and beneficial as I have.

TERMINOLOGY

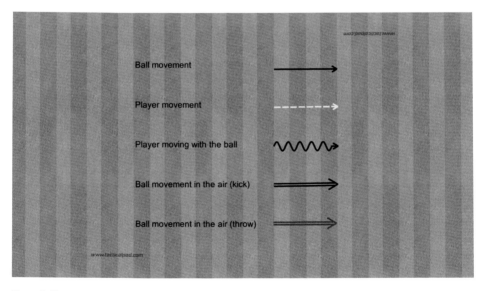

Figure 1. Key to terms.

Scanning: Continuously looking at the bigger picture as opposed to just focusing on the ball: Where is the space? Where is the opposition? Where are my teammates?

Rondos: A variety of possession-based drills that share a common theme of maintaining possession and keeping the ball away from an individual or from a small group who works relentlessly to get the ball

Playmaker: A player who plays for both teams, normally made distinguishable from other players by a different colored bib. They always help the team that has possession of the ball

Wall player: A player who has limited involvement in the practice or game. Wall players tend to be used as additional options for the team in possession to pass to in order to keep the ball

Bonus ball: A second ball added to a practice or game used to add a level of chaos or excitement or simply prolong the activity

Bounce pass: The act of using one touch to immediately return the ball to the player who passed it

Give-and-go: The act of a player passing to another player and then moving to a new area while receiving the ball back from them

Pitch: The area where a game or practice takes place, often referred to as a *field* or *ground*

Praised player: A player the coach highlights for doing something worthy of praise during a scoreboard game and sends to the scoreboard.

Football: Soccer

ENVIRONMENT VS. INSTRUCTION

WHY SCOREBOARD SOCCER?

Scoreboard Soccer is a curriculum that uses environment-based learning to develop young players.

As a coach, I've learned via many different methods, such as coach-education courses, working with others, and countless coaching hours on the pitch. But my coaching experience is only half of my learning journey. My life experience is the other half. Through a previous role, I learned how the environment around us affects our health and well-being and shapes our behavior.

Early in my coaching journey, I planned my sessions on preconceived ideas of what I thought all youth players needed to work on, and my delivery style was very instruction based. Yet I found that this didn't get the best out of my players.

Here are some of the issues I found with taking an instruction-based approach to coaching:

- Coaching points may be dated.

- Information may be misunderstood, misheard, or unheard.

- Instruction may be boring or confusing.

- Invention and creativity may become stifled.

- Players may become dependent on the coach's instructions.

When providing players with a lot of instruction, those players didn't exhibit the behaviors I was hoping for, but rather, often, they exhibited the strong human behavior of defiance. If a young player demonstrates a particular behavior, they likely have a justification for doing so. If you challenge that behavior or decision, they may be more inclined to give you their justification as opposed to listening to your recommendation. A ten-year-old won't be in the headspace of long-term development.

These shortcomings of instruction-based coaching are what led to the creation of Scoreboard Soccer. I realized that creating an effective learning environment could overcome these issues and bring to the surface the behaviors I wanted to see from the players.

Place a row of chairs facing a projector screen, and entering students will automatically sit and look at the screen. You won't need to instruct them. The influence of physical surroundings can have a huge impact, and many organizations have been using this to their advantage for years, subconsciously influencing others to display desired behaviors through the environments they build around people: white lines on the road for us to drive within, tactical product placement in shops to entice us to spend more money, tours of whiskey distilleries conveniently ending in the gift shop, a 10 percent off coupon in hand. This list is extensive. Look around you. Many of your behaviors are programmed, thanks to your environment.

Once I understood this, I started planning sessions by considering the behaviors I wanted to see. As a coach, you may have some priority behaviors you want to develop and bring to the surface during a session. Here is an example of some behaviors I would be keen to encourage and develop in the youth players I work with:

- Running with the ball
- Teamwork
- Passing and moving
- Communication

Now that I know the behaviors I want to see, how can I manipulate the environment to promote, encourage, and praise those behaviors? Scoreboard Soccer provides a platform to do this.

Scoreboard Soccer allows kids to play the game and have fun, and their learning will accelerate when they're enjoying themselves. Also, they'll keep coming back, and over the course of weeks, months, and years, they'll be able to be taught more intricate parts of the game. In my experience, the more time spent using tools such as small-sided games, Scoreboard Soccer, and game-related practices, the more competent players are when we look to implement more complex moments of the game, such as playing out from the back, switching play, and playing through the lines. Don't rush to get to these topics; embrace the journey.

THE BOUNCY CASTLE

WHAT IS SCOREBOARD SOCCER?

Imagine having a group of ten- to fourteen-year-olds, all of different backgrounds, abilities, and attention spans, and trying to coach a session on jumping, teaching them about the benefits to their health and their joints, and asking them to bend their knees, explode off the ground, and jump continuously to improve technique and fitness. How long could you keep the children engaged in that instruction-based environment? Yet, take the instruction away and replace it with a bouncy castle, and I bet they would be much more engaged and enthralled, constantly jumping, laughing, smiling, and exploring—a lot of hidden exercise to improve mental and physical health. I've worked to make Scoreboard Soccer sessions to soccer what a bouncy castle is to jumping.

When developing Scoreboard Soccer and aiming to provide a learning environment conducive for long-term development, I consulted with youth football coaches regarding behaviors they wanted to see in their sessions and what barriers they'd encountered. Table 1 contains a summary of the most common answers.

Table 1 Desired behaviors and common barriers

ENVIRONMENT	BEHAVIORS	BARRIERS
ACTIVITIES AND GAMES TO ALLOW CHILDREN TO PRACTICE AND PLAY FOOTBALL	DRIBBLING	CATERING TO DIFFERENT ABILITY LEVELS
	PASSING	
	CONTROL	KEEPING PLAYERS ENGAGED
PROMOTING BEHAVIORS TO AID LONG-TERM DEVELOPMENT	DEFENDING	
	FINISHING	CATERING TO DIFFERENT FITNESS LEVELS
	RUNNING	
AVOIDING BARRIERS THAT MAY DISRUPT LONG-TERM DEVELOPMENT	DECIDING	
	REACTING	
	TEAMWORK	
	CONFIDENCE	
	SMILING	
	FAILING	
	EXPLORING	
	CREATING	
	RESILIENCE	

My aim was to create environments that would encourage the constant repetition and learning of the behaviours coaches wanted to promote and, at the same time, avoid the common barriers to player development. All these behaviors shown in the table are ever present in the game of football itself. That gave me the starting point for designing my sessions: play the game.

Of course, we can amplify the learning for younger players by reducing area size and numbers on the pitch, to cater to their needs (i.e., play small-sided games [2v2s, 3v3s, and 4v4s]). This is the part of the concept that won't be new to coaches. Small-sided games are a great way to nurture positive behaviors, as they provide goal-scoring opportunities, constant transitions, lots of touches, and loads of activity and fun. Yet where they often fall short is in the "Barriers" column. I found that when playing small-sided games the best player would have the lion's share of the ball. Less-experienced players would have limited time and opportunities on the ball. This meant that some players were in danger of becoming disengaged and uninterested.

Scoreboard Soccer offers a new layer to small-sided games by introducing a fun scoreboard that runs in parallel.

THE SCOREBOARD: A MOTIVATIONAL TEACHING TOOL, RUNNING ALONGSIDE THE GAME

Here is an example of a Scoreboard Soccer game:

Set up two 3v3 small-sided pitches, with three players in red against three players in blue on each pitch. The scoreboard sits in the middle of the two pitches and is simply made up of four red cones and four blue cones. Play 3v3. When a player scores a goal, they come to the side of the pitch (while the game continues) and place a ball on top of one of the cones that match their team's color. Then, the player quickly gets back on the pitch to help the team. The first set of teams (yellows or reds) to fill all four of their cones with balls wins.

This might sound simple, but the kids absolutely love putting a ball on top of the cone. It represents a fun pat on the back from the coach for doing something well and serves as a visual aid to show that the player is helping the team on the way to victory. The player can also see how far along the journey the other team is, which ramps up the competition and the fun.

When Scoreboard Soccer was in its infancy, it was purely meant to be good fun for the young players. But the more I delivered it, the more I found hidden benefits. For example, while a more-talented player was momentarily off the pitch to reward their effort, the other players had an opportunity to increase their involvement in the game, and the standard of my small-sided games in general lifted to a whole new level. Everyone wanted to get on the ball and score to be praised via the fun scoreboards.

But is goal scoring the only behavior worthy of praise in football?

A great way to cater to different ability levels is to praise not only goal scoring but also effort and attitude. Sarah may be a lesser player on the pitch, but when she passes the ball with the inside of her foot and the coach shouts "Fantastic, Sarah! Great pass with the inside of your foot! Come put a ball on the cone!" I can tell you from experience that Sarah will come back onto the pitch desperate to pass with the inside of her foot again. This is the case for all behaviors that you praise through your energy, your enthusiasm, and the scoreboard. In the following pages, I share more about this creative scoreboard. It has become known as Connect Four, and it was one of the first scoreboard games I ever used. There are plenty more to come throughout the book.

CONNECT FOUR

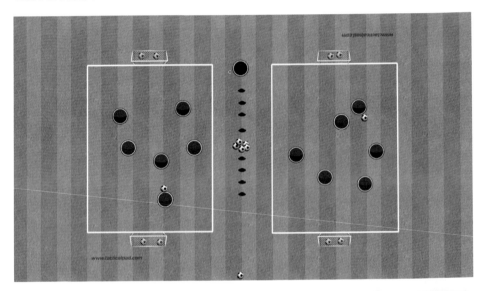

Figure 3. Connect Four setup.

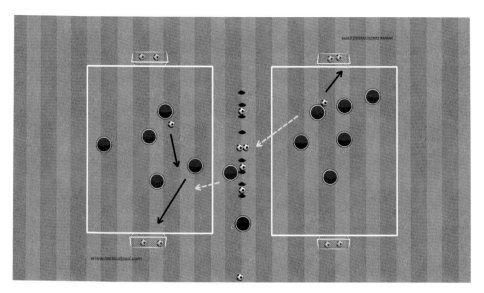

Figure 4. Connect Four in action.

SCOREBOARD GAME

This game consists of two small-sided games with the scoreboard between the pitches. When a team scores a goal, the conceding team collects the ball and immediately continues the game while the goal scorer quickly goes to the scoreboard. But don't send only goal scorers to the scoreboard. Throughout the games, if a player demonstrates positive play or behavior, you as the coach may praise this by saying "Well done" and sending them to the scoreboard.

The scoreboard in this game consists of four blue cones and four red cones, with a supply of balls nearby. The blue set of cones represents the blue scoreboard, and the red set of cones represents the red scoreboard. After a player scores or the coach tells a player to go to the scoreboard due to positive play, the player rushes over and puts a ball on one of their team's colored cones. The first team to fill all four of their cones wins. This game involves collaboration between the teams wearing the same-color bib, and players will work hard because they know factors on the other pitch might result in them losing the game. When a team (both groups of red, for example) fills all four cones, they win the game. At that point, you may choose to reset the scoreboard and add the fun progression that the goal scorer (or praised player) can either put a ball on their team's cone or kick one off the other team's cone.

As always, be sure to let players know you won't reward just goal scoring but also positive behaviors. Rewarding such behaviors will motivate players to repeat them. Scoreboard Soccer is designed to help in the holistic development of young people through praising and promoting characteristics such as teamwork, sportsmanship, and respect.

VARIATIONS

- Frequently varying the following four elements from session to session can help accommodate the number of players and can also combat monotony.

- Modify the number of players.

- Vary whether teams play with a goalkeeper.

- Vary the size or number of goals used.

- Vary whether you run one game or multiple small-sided games simultaneously.

The following are other ways you can vary games from session to session:

- Vary the length or width of the pitch to give players different problems and challenges.

- Introduce more cones at the scoreboard if you wish to prolong games.

- Progress by not only allowing players to add a point to their scoreboard but also allowing them to take one away from the opposition instead.

- Promote player autonomy by choosing captains who can praise players on the opposing team by sending them to the scoreboard.

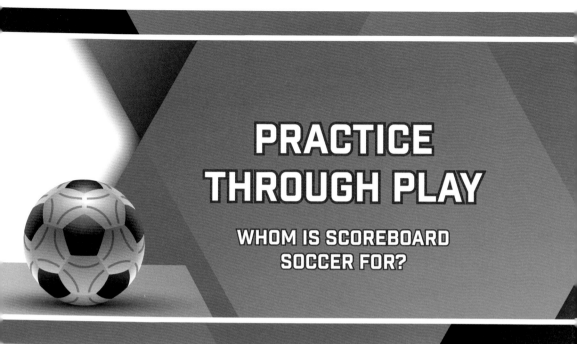

PRACTICE THROUGH PLAY

WHOM IS SCOREBOARD SOCCER FOR?

As a coach, I've found many uses for Scoreboard Soccer. Amid warm-ups, skill practices, game-related practices, conditioned games, and a variety of other coaching content, Scoreboard Soccer is just another delivery method to add to your armory when coaching. In my current capacity as an academy coach, a grassroots coach, and a coach educator, I have used Scoreboard Soccer across many different teams and programs. I have used it during preseason for my adult teams. Small-sided games with competition can be a great workout and a good way to reintroduce players to the ball and football movements. I have used it for academy teams who need something fun and motivational after a heavy defeat. I have used it during school sports programs where I find there's a real mix of ability because it's a good way to challenge and support players of different levels. I'm therefore confident that the content shared throughout this book will be an asset to coaches at any level.

If I were to offer some advice as to who Scoreboard Soccer is most beneficial to, however, it would be for the players who need to play more of the game. All players will develop at different rates, but generally speaking, Scoreboard Soccer is the most ideal for players between the ages of eight and sixteen. There are a lot of players with big gaps in their development simply because they haven't played enough football during this time frame. Speaking as someone who grew up in Scotland, the organic environment for learning to play football in years gone by was street ball. Now that the world has changed and street ball isn't as prevalent, we need to supplement the hours of organized training with time dedicated to playing the game. Scoreboard Soccer is a great way of doing this. Coaches, parents, and guardians are sometimes eager to pinpoint specific things players need to

work on. The player needs to scan more, move the ball quicker, or keep it under control. Sometimes it boils down to them just needing to play more. They need to be constantly exposed to opposition, transition, direction, and problem solving. This, of course, can be surrounded by individual or block practice to hone technique, but it can't be neglected.

Let the players play. Player ownership over learning is crucially important. We learn to ride a bike by riding a bike. We learn to drive a car by driving a car. Let children learn to play football by playing football. As coaches, we are simply the driving instructor giving some guidance and making sure everyone is safe and learning within that environment.

Albert Einstein said it best: "I never teach my pupils, I only provide the conditions in which they can learn." He also said, "Play is the highest form of research," a quote that really resonates with me.

LONG-TERM DEVELOPMENT

WHEN SHOULD I USE SCOREBOARD SOCCER?

Expanding on the recommendation that Scoreboard Soccer would be most suitable for players between the ages of eight and sixteen, I will now discuss when Scoreboard Soccer could be used in a long-term development plan.

As with all the long-term development plans I've designed, it's important to know where you want to go before implementing the steps to get there. It's crucial that coaches recognize that the players in front of us are *people* before they're *players* and that we, as coaches, play an important role in their all-round development. Through their training, they develop not just football skills but also confidence, social skills, and transferrable attributes, such as communication and teamwork, which they can take into other walks of life.

Focusing on football skills for the moment, I have a real passion for ensuring that players are participating in activities that are appropriate for their age and stage of development. I see too many players with gaps in their skill set through rushed development. Parents and guardians are often too eager to have their children play up an age division, and coaches can be too impatient to let kids problem solve through playing the game. I know plenty of coaches who preach long-term development but neglect practicing it after four or five heavy defeats.[1]

---

1. What's your definition of *defeat*? Losing 10–0 in a development game for nine-year-olds or giving up on their long-term development as a result?

For the players I work with, I simplify the phases into three simple stages:

1. Love Football

2. Play Football

3. Learn Football

And there's natural overlap between the three.

When faced with a group of players, I try my best to identify what phase they are in and implement appropriate sessions to accommodate their needs and best prepare them for the next stage. For example, with players within the age range of four to twelve, I find it's crucial to develop a love for football, a love that may last a lifetime.

Once players have developed a love for the game, I look to give them a platform to play the game, allowing me to assess how far they can take themselves as players and what interventions I may need to make to further support them. Here are the key stages of a youth player's development with the curriculums I deliver at each stage:

- Love Football: Storybook Soccer

- Play Football: Scoreboard Soccer

- Learn Football: Strategy Soccer

I deliver Scoreboard Soccer when players have already developed a passion for the game and are comfortably believing that football training is a fun, safe, and nurturing environment to be in. Scoreboard Soccer can then help give players a strong foundation of technical skills, game-based movements, and problem solving. Once this foundation has been formed, players are better equipped to learn and implement more-complicated parts of the game through my Strategy Soccer curriculum, which delves deeper into styles of play, formations, and tactics. In my experience, the more time spent in the Scoreboard Soccer phase, the higher quality that's displayed during future training. On the flip side, I've seen a lot of frustrated coaches working with 15- and 16-year-olds who aren't performing what's being asked of them to the quality demanded from the coach, because they were rushed through earlier stages of the development process.

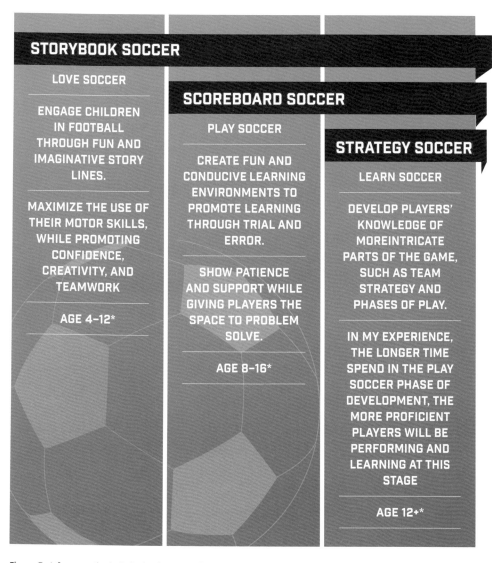

STORYBOOK SOCCER

LOVE SOCCER

ENGAGE CHILDREN IN FOOTBALL THROUGH FUN AND IMAGINATIVE STORY LINES.

MAXIMIZE THE USE OF THEIR MOTOR SKILLS, WHILE PROMOTING CONFIDENCE, CREATIVITY, AND TEAMWORK

AGE 4–12*

SCOREBOARD SOCCER

PLAY SOCCER

CREATE FUN AND CONDUCIVE LEARNING ENVIRONMENTS TO PROMOTE LEARNING THROUGH TRIAL AND ERROR.

SHOW PATIENCE AND SUPPORT WHILE GIVING PLAYERS THE SPACE TO PROBLEM SOLVE.

AGE 8–16*

STRATEGY SOCCER

LEARN SOCCER

DEVELOP PLAYERS' KNOWLEDGE OF MOREINTRICATE PARTS OF THE GAME, SUCH AS TEAM STRATEGY AND PHASES OF PLAY.

IN MY EXPERIENCE, THE LONGER TIME SPEND IN THE PLAY SOCCER PHASE OF DEVELOPMENT, THE MORE PROFICIENT PLAYERS WILL BE PERFORMING AND LEARNING AT THIS STAGE

AGE 12+*

Figure 5. A focus on the holistic development of the person and on having fun should be paramount throughout.

*Players develop at different speeds; however, I'm identifying the ages I find myself delivering each curriculum to. You'll notice an overlap of suggested age groups, and crucially, there's an overlap of the key outcomes. Loving, playing, and learning football all go hand-in-hand throughout a player's journey.

ENCOURAGE EFFORT

HOW DO I DELIVER SCOREBOARD SOCCER EFFECTIVELY?

For players and coaches alike, practice makes perfect. In my own experience, the countless hours spent designing, delivering, and refining sessions have been the biggest factor in my development as a coach. Players learn by playing; coaches learn by coaching.

In regard to delivering Scoreboard Soccer, there are a few things I strongly advise, but these tips by no means apply exclusively to Scoreboard games. They apply to working with children in general.

Be enthusiastic. Enthusiastic body language and the way you use your voice and your energy throughout the session will transfer to the young players you're working with. They'll mirror your enthusiasm and will unfortunately also mirror any negativity. I know it's challenging—coaches often work second jobs, have families, and deliver multiple sessions each week. These stressors and other factors can drain our energy, but it's important to remember that Kyle, one of your players, only sees you for that one hour a week. He doesn't know that you're exhausted from a long workday and a sleepless night.

Be the best part of the players' week. While Kyle won't know the stressors in your life, often, we don't know everything that's going on in a player's life. Football training might be the best couple of hours of Rosa's week, due to issues at home or school. As a result, she may seem disengaged, or her mind may drift. Be ready to cut kids some slack, and for those who are disruptive or "attention seeking," maybe it's because they do need some attention.

When delivering Scoreboard Soccer, it's beneficial to involve players in the delivery of the games. Once you have a good grasp on delivering with energy, enthusiasm, and patience, it's a great time to give players some autonomy in regard to setting up, picking teams, or designing the scoreboards. Some of the scoreboard games in this book have been designed and delivered by the players themselves, and I can't stress enough the importance and satisfaction of developing good people as well as good players.

Encourage effort. It's important that the players understand that you value effort more so than the outcome. If you put a high value on effort through praise and using the scoreboard, effort is what players will continue to demonstrate, and the outcomes will improve. For example, if you praise a player via the scoreboard for shooting, even if the shot was unsuccessful, they will continue to have the confidence to shoot the ball. The outcome (scoring goals) is then more likely to improve through practice.

Figure 6. Ways to develop player autonomy

"I have to tell you that Thomas played on at least thirty different teams over the years for at least twenty-five different coaches between his soccer, baseball, basketball, rugby, and wrestling teams. You remain his favorite coach from among all those guys, and soccer became his favourite sport while he was playing for you.

"And that's pretty much a unanimous opinion among the players. They all say you were the best. You had that perfect balance of working them hard while teaching them skills and yet still making it fun. You're a rock star to them."[2]

---

2. Email from a parent, with the player's name changed

THE CONTENT

TECHNICAL GAMES

Small-sided games with a scoreboard, used to develop technical skills.

TECHNICAL GAME 1: PASSING

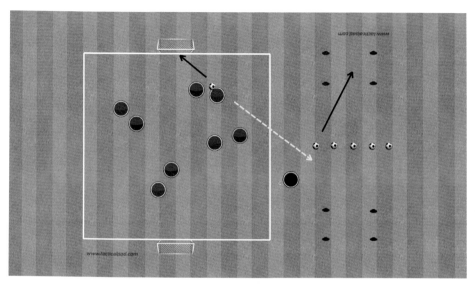

Figure 7. The goal scorer quickly leaves the game to attempt to score on the scoreboard, using a ball outside the pitch.

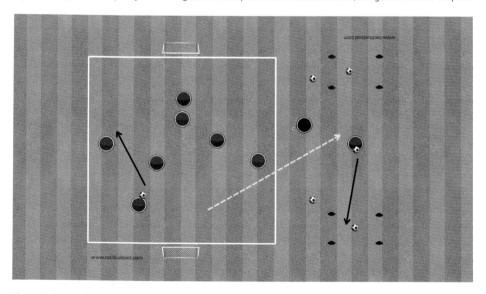

Figure 8. The coach can reward a player for positive behavior by sending them to the scoreboard as well. If possible, a second coach can help players at the scoreboard. This is the case for all scoreboard games.

SCOREBOARD GAME—PASSING

When a player scores a goal, the conceding team collects the ball and immediately continues the game while the goal scorer quickly goes to the scoreboard and attempts to get a team scoreboard goal by completing a passing challenge.

The scoreboard in this game consists of two five-by-five-yard boxes. One box represents the red team's scoreboard, and the other represents the blue team's scoreboard. After scoring a goal in the 4v4 game, the goal scorer rushes to the scoreboard side of the pitch and has one attempt to pass a ball from a central passing zone into the scoreboard for their team. If the pass stops inside the scoreboard, it's a point for that team; however, any balls landing outside a scoreboard remain in play for a future rewarded player to attempt to pass into the scoreboard for their team. When all balls are in the scoreboard, the game is over, and teams count to see who has won, then reset the scoreboard to play again. At that point, you may want to mix up the teams or, if you have more than one pitch running at the same time, alternate opposition for the players.

Be sure to let players know that you won't reward just goal scoring but also positive behaviors, such as creativity and communication, by sending them to the scoreboard. Rewarding such behaviors will motivate players to repeat them. Since this scoreboard's focus is passing, you might encourage and praise this during the small-sided games. The scoreboard can also give coaches an opportunity to coach passing technique on an individual basis.

VARIATIONS

- Frequently varying the following four elements from session to session can help accommodate the number of players you have at your session and can also combat monotony.

- Modify the number of players.

- Vary whether teams play with a goalkeeper.

- Vary the size or number of goals used.

- Vary whether you run one game or multiple small-sided games simultaneously.

The following are other ways you can vary games from session to session:

- Vary the length or width of the pitch to give the players different problems and challenges.

- Increase or decrease the distance of the pass, to support or challenge players.

- Increase or decrease the size of the scoreboard, to support or challenge players.

- Challenge players to pass with their nondominant foot, to encourage passing proficiency with both feet.

- Set a time limit on the game, and whichever team has the most soccer balls in their scoreboard when time runs out wins.

- Progress the game such that a team wins by having all the balls in their scoreboard, allowing players to start to pass from the opponent's scoreboard into theirs.

TECHNICAL GAME 2: DRIBBLING

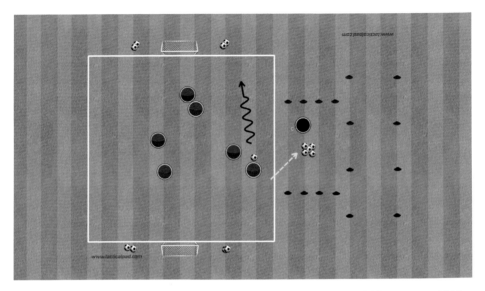

Figure 9. Once a player scores (or is affirmed for positive behavior), the player exits the field to attempt a dribbling challenge

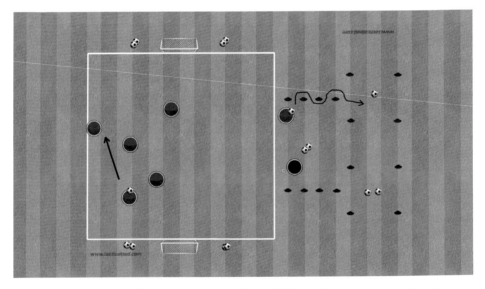

Figure 10. While the rewarded player is at the scoreboard doing a dribbling challenge, their team continues the game, using a ball from beside that team's goal.

SCOREBOARD GAME—DRIBBLING

When a player scores a goal, someone else on the scoring team collects a ball from beside the team's goal, and the team immediately continues the game while the goal scorer quickly goes to the scoreboard to attempt a scoreboard goal for their team by completing a dribbling challenge.

The scoreboard in this game consists of two three-by-three-yard boxes. One box represents the red team's scoreboard, and the other represents the blue team's scoreboard. After scoring a goal in the 3v3 game, the goal scorer rushes to the scoreboard side of the pitch and has one attempt to dribble a ball through a line of cones and into the scoreboard for their team. If the player bumps a cone before reaching the scoreboard, the player must return the ball to the central pile and rejoin the game without scoring that point. Players need to find the balance of dribbling fast to score and quickly get back onto the pitch to help the team and also not rushing and losing control of the ball. When all balls are in the scoreboard, the game is over, and teams count to see who wins, then resets the scoreboard to play again. At that point, you may want to mix up the teams or, if you have more than one pitch running at the same time, alternate opposition for the players.

Be sure to let players know that you won't reward just goal scoring but also positive **behaviors**, such as passing and teamwork, by sending them to the scoreboard. Rewarding such behaviors will motivate players to repeat them. As this scoreboard's focus is dribbling, you might encourage and praise this during the small-sided games. The scoreboard can also give coaches an opportunity to coach dribbling technique on an individual basis.

VARIATIONS

- Frequently varying the following four elements from session to session can help accommodate the number of players you have at your session and can also combat monotony.

- Modify the number of players.

- Vary whether teams play with a goalkeeper.

- Vary the size or number of the goals used.

- Vary whether you run one game or multiple small-sided games simultaneously.

The following are other ways you can vary games from session to session:

- Vary the length or width of the pitch to give the players different problems and challenges.

- Increase or decrease the distance between the cones, to support or challenge players.

- Challenge players to dribble with their nondominant foot, to encourage dribbling proficiency with both feet.

- Set a time limit on the game, and whichever team has the most balls in their scoreboard when time runs out wins.

- Progress the game such that players can steal balls from the opposition's scoreboard when all balls are gone from the central pile.

TECHNICAL GAME 3: CONTROL

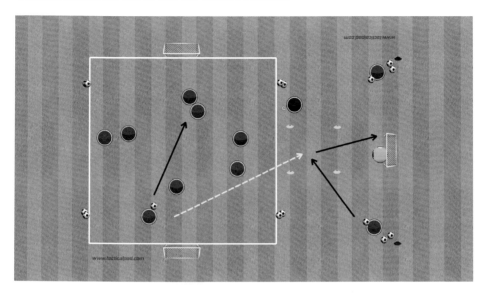

Figure 11. Once a player scores or is sent to the scoreboard for positive behavior, a feeder passes the ball to them and they attempt to control the ball in the box and then score a goal.

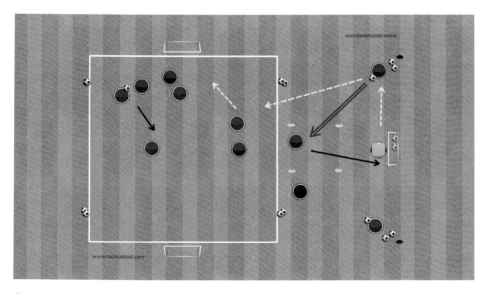

Figure 12. Once a player shoots at the scoreboard goal, they replace the feeder for their team, and the feeder joins the game in progress.

SCOREBOARD GAME—CONTROL

When a player scores a goal, the conceding team collects a ball from the side of the pitch and immediately continues the game while the goal scorer quickly goes to the scoreboard and attempts to get a goal for their team by completing a control challenge.

The scoreboard in this game consists of a six-by-side-yard box, a ball feeder, a large goal, and a goalkeeper. After scoring a goal in the game, the goal scorer rushes to the box and receives a pass from the feeder on their team. The goal scorer from the game has one attempt to control the ball within the box and then shoot on goal. If they score, the team receives a reward of a bonus goal on top of the current score from the small-sided game. The shooting player will now swap places with the feeder, who rushes to join the game. Play for a set time limit before resetting the scoreboard to play again. At that point, you may want to mix up the teams or, if you have more than one pitch running at the same time, alternate opposition for the players.

Be sure to let players know that you won't reward just goal scoring but also positive behaviors, such as shielding the ball and praising the efforts of teammates, by sending them to the scoreboard. Rewarding such behaviors will motivate players to repeat them. As this scoreboard's focus is control, you might encourage and praise this during the small-sided games. The scoreboard can also give coaches an opportunity to coach control technique on an individual basis.

- Frequently varying the following four elements from session to session can help accommodate the number of players you have at your session and can also combat monotony.

- Modify the number of players.

- Vary whether the teams play with a goalkeeper.

- Vary the size or number of goals used.

- Vary whether you run one game or multiple small-sided games simultaneously.

The following are other ways you can vary games from session to session:

- Vary the length or width of the pitch to give the players different problems and challenges.

- Increase or decrease the distance of the feed, to support or challenge players.

- Increase or decrease the size of the box players must control the ball in before shooting to support or challenge players.

- Ask feeders to throw the ball in the air so their teammates can work on control with different parts of the body.

- Rotate who the goalkeeper is within the game.

- Play to a set number of goals from the scoreboard to win the game.

TECHNICAL GAME 4: SHOOTING

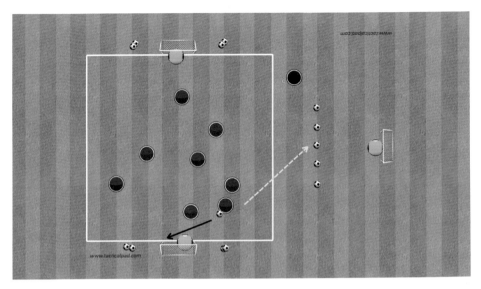

Figure 13. The goal-scoring or otherwise-rewarded player has one chance to score on the scoreboard goal.

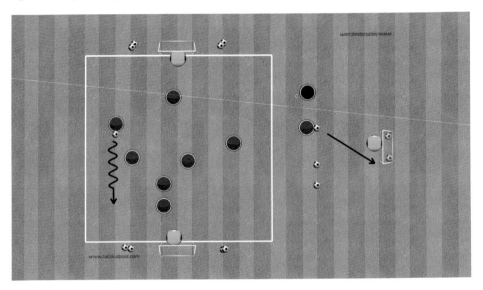

Figure 14. In one variant, the player who scores may continue shooting until they miss. Alternatively you can support players by allowing them to continue shooting until they score.

SCOREBOARD GAME—SHOOTING

When a player scores a goal, the conceding team collects a ball from beside their goal and immediately continues the game while the goal scorer quickly goes to the scoreboard to attempt to get a goal for their team by completing a shooting challenge.

The scoreboard in this game consists of a line of balls in a shooting zone, a large goal, and a goalkeeper. After scoring a goal in the game, the goal scorer rushes to the shooting zone and tries to score against the scoreboard goalkeeper. That player has one attempt to shoot and get a point for scoring. If the player misses, they must return the ball to the shooting zone before being able to rejoin the game. If the player scores, the team receives a bonus goal on top of the current score line from the small-sided game. Play for a set time limit before resetting the scoreboard to play again. At that point, you may want to mix up the teams if you have more than one pitch running at the same time or alternate opposition for the players.

Be sure to let players know that you won't reward just goal scoring but also positive behaviors, such as turning with the ball and playing with confidence, by sending them to the scoreboard. Rewarding such behaviors will motivate players to repeat them. As this scoreboard's focus is shooting, you might encourage and praise this during the small-sided games. The scoreboard can also give coaches an opportunity to coach shooting technique on an individual basis.

- Frequently varying the following four elements from session to session can help accommodate the number of players you have at your session and can also combat monotony.

- Modify the number of players.

- Vary whether the teams play with a goalkeeper.

- Vary the size or number of goals used.

- Vary whether you run one game or multiple small-sided games simultaneously.

The following are other ways you can vary games from session to session:

- Vary the length or width of the pitch to give the players different problems and challenges.

- Increase or decrease the distance of the shot, to support or challenge players.

- Challenge players to hit a moving ball by taking a touch before striking, or perhaps have a coach throw the ball in to play.

- Rotate who the goalkeeper is within the game.

- If a player scores a shot, allow them to keep taking bonus shots for goals until they miss.

- Set out eleven balls and establish that the game will be over when they're all in the net; the team who put the most balls in the net wins.

TECHNICAL GAME 5: 1V1s

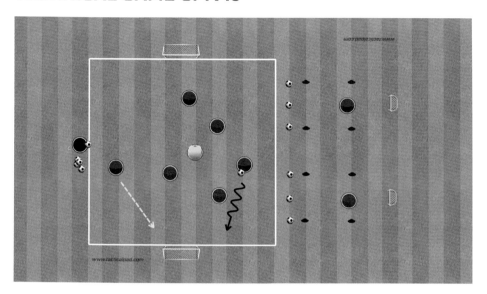

Figure 15. This scoreboard consists of players attempting to beat an opposing player in a 1v1 situation. The defenders can deny that player a point by not allowing them through the scoreboard.

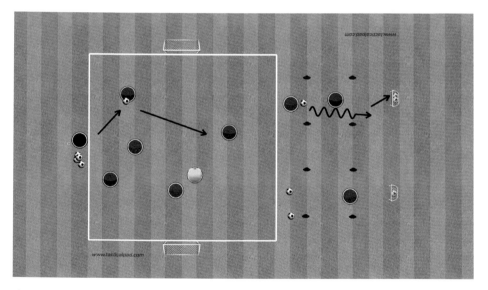

Figure 16. A player sent to the scoreboard side of the pitch works to drive the ball through the channel and past a defender to add a point to the team's score.

SCOREBOARD GAME—1V1s

When a player scores a goal, the coach passes in a new ball, and the teams immediately continue the game while the goal scorer quickly goes to the scoreboard and attempts to get a goal for their team by completing a 1v1 challenge. The playmaker in yellow in figures 15 and 16 is optional. When needed, a playmaker plays for whichever team is in possession, playing for both teams throughout the game.

The scoreboard in this game consists of two 1v1 areas, each fifteen by twelve yards, featuring a supply of balls where players approach the channels. A defender from each team starts in line with the cones at the back of the opposing team's channel. After scoring a goal in the game, the goal scorer rushes to the team's channel and attempts to get through the channel and past the opposition's defender. The defender becomes live once the attacker enters the channel. The attacker has one attempt to get past the defender. If the attacker is successful, a goal is added to the score of the game. If the defender prevents the attacker from getting through the channel, the defender's team scores a goal. Play first to a set number of goals, totaling the goals from the game and the 1v1 challenge. Then reset the scoreboard to play again. At that point, you may want to mix up the teams or, if you have more than one pitch running at the same time, alternate opposition for the players. You might also change the defenders for each team.

Be sure to let players know that you won't reward just goal scoring but also positive behaviors, such as tackling and effort, by sending them to the scoreboard. Rewarding such behaviors will motivate players to repeat them. As this scoreboard's focus is 1v1 attacking and defending, you might encourage and praise this during the small-sided games. The scoreboard can also give coaches an opportunity to coach 1v1 attacking and defending on an individual basis.

- Frequently varying the following four elements from session to session can help accommodate the number of players you have at your session and can also combat monotony.

- Modify the number of players.

- Vary whether teams play with a goalkeeper.

- Vary the size or number of goals used.

- Vary whether you run one game or multiple small-sided games simultaneously.

The following are other ways you can vary games from session to session:

- Vary the length or width of the pitch to give the players different problems and challenges.

- Increase or decrease the size of the channel, to support or challenge players.

- Reward a bonus goal to defenders who not only win the ball but then drive outside the channel with possession of the ball, encouraging quick transition.

- Rotate who the defenders are within the channels.

- Rotate through any playmakers used frequently.

- Progress to allowing attackers who get past the defenders to have a shot on goal.

- Play first to a certain number of attacking successes in 1v1 situations at the scoreboards.

TECHNICAL GAME 6: GOALKEEPER DISTRIBUTION

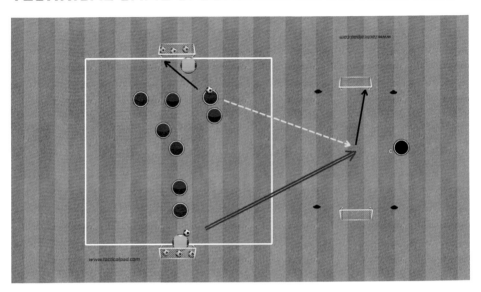

Figure 17. As soon as a player scores, they rush to the small pitch to receive a pass from the goalkeeper and attempt to score on the small pitch.

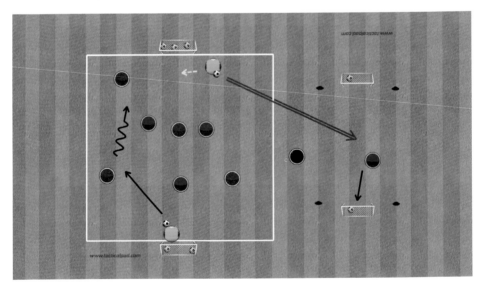

Figure 18. While a goal scorer is busy on the small pitch and that team's goalkeeper is distracted focusing on distribution, the opposing team can take advantage of their temporary overload and attempt to score in the game.

SCOREBOARD GAME—GOALKEEPER DISTRIBUTION

When a player scores a goal, the conceding team collects the ball and immediately continues the game while the goal scorer quickly goes to the scoreboard and attempts to get a goal for their team by completing a distribution challenge.

The scoreboard in this game consists of a small pitch with two goals. After someone scores a goal in the game, the goalkeeper of the scoring team quickly grabs a ball from that team's goal and works on their distribution of the ball, by playing a pass to the goal scorer, who rushes to the small pitch. The goal scorer attempts to quickly receive the ball from the goalkeeper and score a bonus goal on the small pitch. This must all be done with as much pace and quality, as the game resumes immediately, with the opposition trying to take advantage of their momentary overload on the pitch and the briefly distracted goalkeeper, who's working on distribution. Play first to a set number of goals, totaling the goals from the game and the goalkeeper-distribution challenge.

Be sure to let players know that you won't reward just goal scoring but also positive behaviors, such as keeping possession and creating space for others through movement off the ball, by sending them to the scoreboard. Rewarding such behaviors will motivate players to repeat them. As this scoreboard's focus is goalkeeper distribution, the more you praise outfield players and send them to the scoreboard, the more the goalkeeper gets to react to this and work on their distribution. The scoreboard can also give coaches an opportunity to coach receiving the ball back to goal, turning, and finishing.

VARIATIONS

- Modify the number of players and the size of goals depending on how many players you have and the age and stage of the group.

- Vary the length or width of the pitch from session to session to give the players different problems and challenges.

- Ask, challenge, and coach the goalkeepers to vary their distribution, through kicking, throwing, or rolling the ball.

- Rotate through the goalkeepers within the game if your team doesn't have a set goalkeeper and other players want to work on this position.

TECHNICAL GAME 7: LONG PASSING

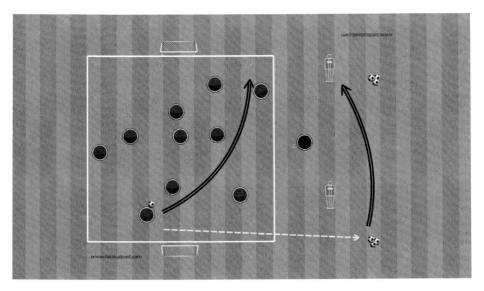

Figure 19. The player rushing off the pitch has one attempt to hit the far-away mannequin from behind the close mannequin.

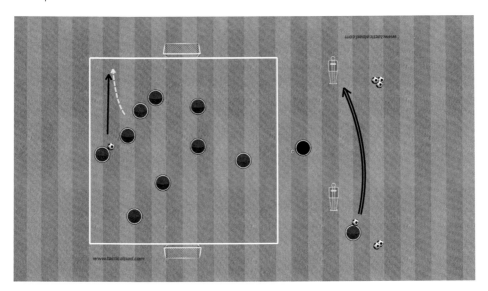

Figure 20. You can reward players for positive behaviors, such as assists.

When a player scores a goal, the conceding team collects the ball and immediately continues the game while the goal scorer quickly goes to the scoreboard and attempts to get a goal for their team by completing a long-passing challenge.

The scoreboard in this game consists of two mannequins about thirty yards apart (vary depending on the players' age and stage). After scoring a goal in the game, the goal scorer rushes to collect a ball near the mannequins and aims to play a long pass from anywhere behind one mannequin to hit the other. The goal scorer has one attempt to hit the mannequin, which would result in adding a goal to the score of the game. First, play to a set number of goals, with the goals from the game and the long-pass challenge both counting. Then reset the scoreboard to play again. At that point, you may want to mix up the teams or, if you have more than one pitch running at the same time, alternate opposition for the players. You may also increase or decrease the distance of the mannequins, depending on how much success the players are having.

Be sure to let players know that you won't reward just goal scoring but also positive behaviors, such as assisting goals and determination, by sending them to the scoreboard. Rewarding such behaviors will motivate players to repeat them. As this scoreboard's focus is long passing, you might encourage and praise this during the small-sided games. The scoreboard can also give coaches an opportunity to coach long-pass attacking on an individual basis.

- Frequently varying the following four elements from session to session can help accommodate the number of players you have at your session and can also combat monotony.

- Modify the number of players.

- Vary whether teams play with a goalkeeper.

- Vary the size or number of goals used.

- Vary whether you run one game or multiple small-sided games simultaneously.

- Vary the length or width of the pitch to give the players different problems and challenges.

- Increase or decrease the distance of the long pass, to support or challenge players.

- Vary the long-pass technique, encouraging or coaching driven, lofted, or aerial passes.

- Depending on space and equipment, you may be able to set up multiple targets for the long pass, where hitting the farthest targets achieves the most points.

TECHNICAL GAME 8: CROSSING

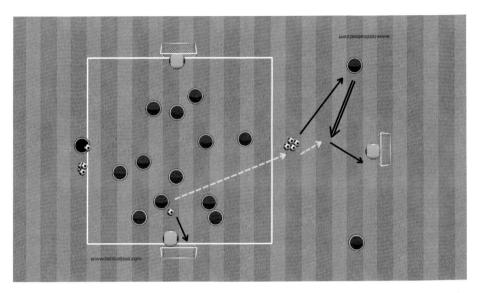

Figure 21. As soon as a player scores, they rush to the scoreboard and pass to the same-team crosser, who passes the ball back to them, and they then attempt to score a bonus point.

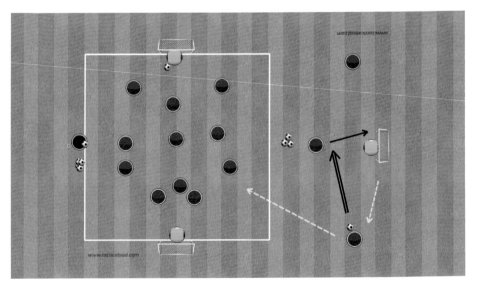

Figure 22. After the crosser has passed the ball to the player who just came off the pitch, the crosser joins the game, and the other player becomes the crosser.

SCOREBOARD GAME—CROSSING

When a player scores a goal, the coach passes in a new ball, and teams immediately continue the game while the goal scorer quickly goes to the scoreboard and attempts to get a goal for their team by completing a crossing challenge.

The scoreboard in this game consists of two crossers (one from each team), a pile of balls, and a goalkeeper. After scoring a goal in the game, the goal scorer rushes to the pile of balls positioned such that a ball can be easily passed to the crosser on that team. After passing the ball to the crosser, the player looks to get in a position to receive a cross and try to score a goal for the team. First, play to a set number of goals, totaling the goals from the game and the crossing challenge. The rotation shown in figure 22 shows the player who attacks the cross then becoming the crosser and the crosser quickly joining the game after crossing the ball; however, you may want to keep a certain player as the crossers if this is something you're looking to develop in them.

Be sure to let players know that you won't reward just goal scoring but also positive behaviors, such as foot skills and determination, by sending them to the scoreboard. Rewarding such behaviors will motivate players to repeat them. As this scoreboard's focus is crossing, you might encourage and praise this during the small-sided games. The scoreboard can also give coaches an opportunity to coach crossing on an individual basis.

VARIATIONS

- Frequently varying the following four elements from session to session can help accommodate the number of players you have at your session and can also combat monotony.

- Modify the number of players.

- Vary whether teams play with a goalkeeper.

- Vary the size or number of goals used.

- Vary whether you run one game or multiple small-sided games simultaneously.

- Vary the length or width of the pitch to give the players different problems and challenges.

- Progress the scoreboard by allowing the crossing player from the opposition to step in and defend against the crosser of the team trying to get a bonus point at the scoreboard, creating a 1v1 battle during the crossing situation.

TECHNICAL GAME 9: VOLLEYS

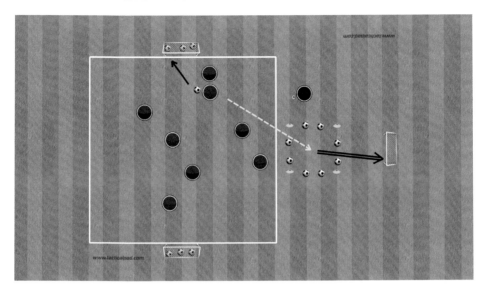

Figure 23. A player sent off the pitch gets one volley attempt before rejoining the game still in progress.

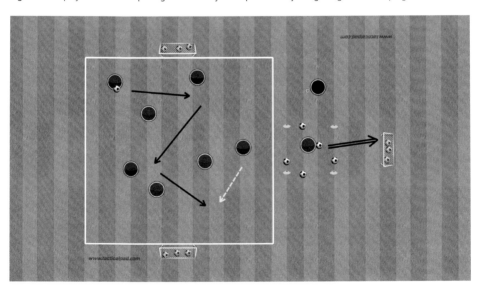

Figure 24. If you do not have a goalkeeper at the scoreboard, you could stipulate a point is only awarded if the volley reaches the goal without bouncing.

SCOREBOARD GAME—VOLLEYS

When a player scores a goal, the conceding team collects the ball and immediately continues the game while the goal scorer quickly goes to the scoreboard and attempts to get a goal for their team by completing a volley challenge.

The scoreboard in this game consists of a shooting area marked out by four cones and a supply of balls around the area. After scoring a goal in the game, the goal scorer rushes to the shooting area and attempts to score a volley into the goalkeeper. This can be done by throwing the ball into the air or flicking it up with one's foot before striking the volley. The player has one attempt to get the ball past the goalkeeper, which would result in adding a goal to the score of the game. Play for a set amount of time, and whichever team has the most combined goals from the game and the scoreboard wins. Then reset the scoreboard to play again. At that point, you may want to mix up the teams or, if you have more than one pitch running at the same time, alternate opposition for the players.

Be sure to let players know that you won't reward just goal scoring but also positive behaviors, such as running back to help your team defend and team spirit, by sending them to the scoreboard. Rewarding such behaviors will motivate players to repeat them. As this scoreboard's focus is volleying attacks, you might encourage and praise this during the small-sided games. The scoreboard can also give coaches an opportunity to coach volleys on an individual basis.

- Frequently varying the following four elements from session to session can help accommodate the number of players you have at your session and can also combat monotony.

- Modify the number of players.

- Vary whether teams play with a goalkeeper.

- Vary the size or number of goals used.

- Vary whether you run one game or multiple small-sided games simultaneously.

The following are other ways you can vary games from session to session:

- Vary the length or width of the pitch to give the players different problems and challenges.

- Increase or decrease the size of the shooting area.

- If you don't have a goalkeeper for the volley challenge, perhaps use targets in the goal or give two goals for players scoring off the post, to work on shooting in the corners.

- Stipulate that it must be a full volley (no bounce) or allow the players to hit a half volley (the ball can bounce before striking).

- Increase the difficulty of striking the volley by having a coach feed the ball in, either by hand or by kicking it.

- First, play to a certain number of successful volleys at the scoreboards, then add emphasis on rewarding scoring or positive behaviors in the game.

TECHNICAL GAME 10: DISGUISE

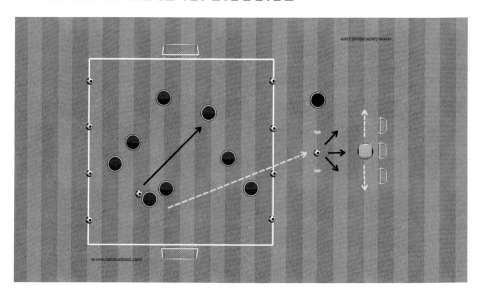

Figure 25. A player who rushes off the pitch has one attempt to use disguised passing to score on one of three guarded mini goals.

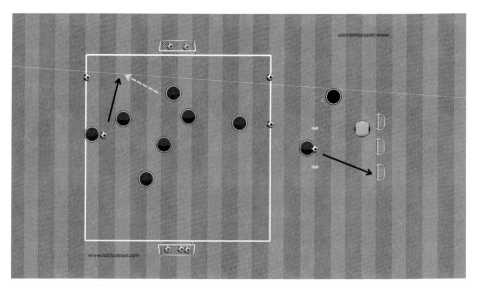

Figure 26. The player may look to pass into one of the many goals before playing a disguised pass into another.

58

SCOREBOARD GAME—DISGUISE

When a player scores a goal, the conceding team collects a ball from the side of the pitch and immediately continues the game while the goal scorer quickly goes to the scoreboard and attempts to get a goal for their team by completing a disguise challenge.

The scoreboard in this game consists of a passing area and three mini goals guarded by a player (you might want to use a goalkeeper). After scoring a goal in the game, the goal scorer rushes to the mini goals and attempts to pass a ball into one of the goals, working on disguised passing. First, play to a set number of goals, totaling the goals from the game and the disguise challenge. Then reset the score to play again. At that point, you may want to mix up the teams or, if you have more than one pitch running at the same time, alternate opposition for the players. You may also want to rotate who the defender of the mini goals is.

Be sure to let players know that you won't reward just goal scoring but also positive behaviors, such as overlapping and unpredictable attacking play, by sending them to the scoreboard. Rewarding such behaviors will motivate players to repeat them. As this scoreboard's focus is disguise, you might encourage and praise this during the small-sided games. The scoreboard can also give coaches an opportunity to coach disguised passing on an individual basis.

- Frequently varying the following four elements from session to session can help accommodate the number of players you have at your session and can also combat monotony.

- Modify the number of players.

- Vary whether teams play with a goalkeeper.

- Vary the size or number of goals used.

- Vary whether you run one game or multiple small-sided games simultaneously.

The following are other ways you can vary games from session to session:

- Vary the length or width of the pitch to give the players different problems and challenges.

- Increase or decrease the number of target goals at the scoreboard, to support or challenge players.

- Increase or decrease the distance of the target goals at the scoreboard, to support or challenge players.

- If a well-disguised pass leads to a goal in the game, praise this by awarding two goals.

- Progress to using a defender to make the scoreboard 1v1, with the attacker looking to utilize disguise to score in one of the three mini goals. Encourage faking to pass one way before going the other or faking to pass before dribbling past the defender to score.

TECHNICAL GAME 11: THROW-INS

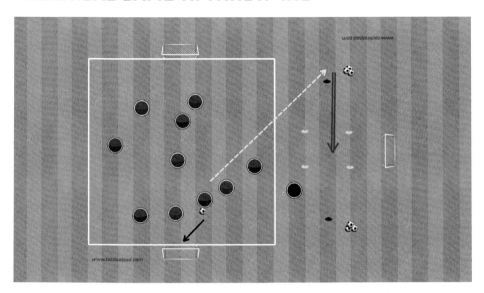

Figure 27. A goal-scoring player rushes off the pitch to balls designated for their team and attempts a throw-in into the box.

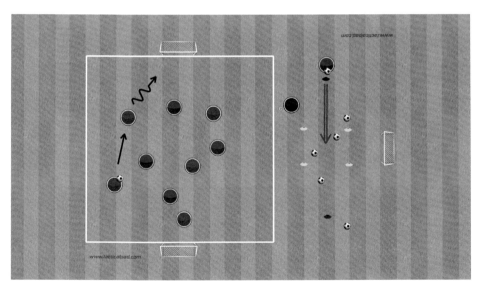

Figure 28. A reminder that a second coach could be used to work on a players technique at the scoreboards.

SCOREBOARD GAME—THROW-INS

When a player scores a goal, the scoring team collects a ball from beside their goal and immediately continues the game while the goal scorer quickly goes to the scoreboard and attempts to get a goal for their team by completing a throw-in challenge.

The scoreboard in this game consists of a five-by-five-yard box that the goal scorer must bounce the ball into using the throw-in technique. The coach can determine the distance from which the player needs to throw, depending on the player's age and stage. After scoring a goal in the game, the goal scorer rushes to balls designated for their team, collects one and attempts to bounce the ball into the box with a throw-in. The player has one attempt, and if the player is successful, a goal is added to the team's score in the game. The coach should be on hand to judge the throw-in technique and ensure that it's within the laws of the game. Players may also need feedback and help to work on their throw-ins while at the scoreboard. First, play to a set number of successful throw-ins that land in the box. Then reset the scoreboard to play again. At that point, you might want to mix up the teams or, if you have more than one pitch running at the same time, alternate opposition for the players.

Be sure to let players know that you won't reward just goal scoring but also positive behaviors, such as players rotating around the field and being unpredictable, by sending them to the scoreboard. Rewarding such behaviors will motivate players to repeat them. As this scoreboard's focus is throw-ins, you might encourage and praise this during the small-sided games. The scoreboard can also give coaches an opportunity to coach throw-in technique on an individual basis.

VARIATIONS

- Frequently varying the following four elements from session to session can help accommodate the number of players you have at your session and can also combat monotony.

- Modify the number of players.

- Vary whether teams play with a goalkeeper.

- Vary the size or number of goals used.

- Vary whether you run one game or multiple small-sided games simultaneously.

The following are other ways you can vary games from session to session:

- Vary the length or width of the pitch to give the players different problems and challenges.

- Increase or decrease the size of the box players are aiming for at the scoreboard, to support or challenge players.

- Increase or decrease the distance of the throw-in, to support or challenge players.

- Replace the box with a player who must control and shoot from the throw-in, to allow players to practice throwing the ball to teammates.

TECHNICAL GAME 12: PANENKA

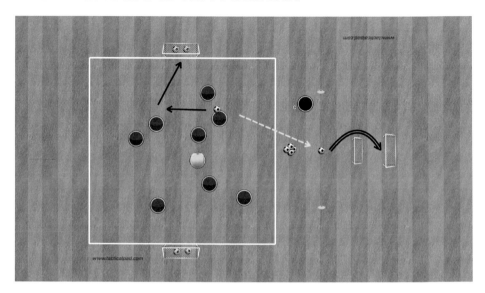

Figure 29. A scoring player rushes off the pitch and attempts to loft a ball over one goal and into another (Panenka).

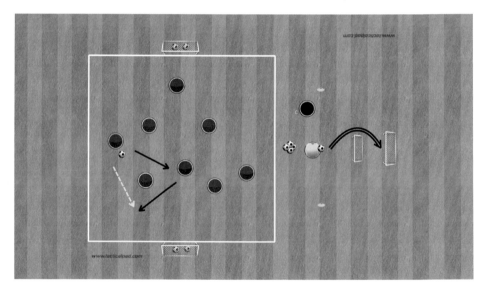

Figure 30. The playmaker can be the player sent off the field to attempt a Panenka.

SCOREBOARD GAME—PANENKA

The playmaker in yellow in figures 29 and 30 is optional. When a player scores a goal, the conceding team immediately continues the game while the goal scorer quickly goes to the scoreboard and attempts to get a goal for their team by completing a Panenka challenge.

The scoreboard in this game consists of a supply of balls and two small goals, with one placed five yards behind the other. After scoring a goal in the game, the goal scorer rushes to the scoreboard and attempts to loft the ball over the first small goal and have it land in the second for a point. Play for a set time limit, and the team with the most combined goals from the game and the scoreboard wins. Then reset the scoreboard to play again. At that point, you may want to mix up the teams or, if you have more than one pitch running at the same time, alternate opposition for the players.

Be sure to let players know that you won't reward just goal scoring but also positive behaviors, such as a good first touch of the ball and never giving up, by sending them to the scoreboard. Rewarding such behaviors will motivate players to repeat them. As this scoreboard's focus is the Panenka technique of lofting the ball in a disguised fashion, you might encourage and praise this during the small-sided games. The scoreboard can also give coaches an opportunity to coach the Panenka on an individual basis.

VARIATIONS

- Frequently varying the following four elements from session to session can help accommodate the number of players you have at your session and can also combat monotony.

- Modify the number of players.

- Vary whether teams play with a goalkeeper.

- Vary the size or number of goals used.

- Vary whether you run one game or multiple small-sided games simultaneously.

The following are other ways you can vary games from session to session:

- Vary the length or width of the pitch to give the players different problems and challenges.

- Increase or decrease the distance to and between the mini goals.

- Implement a scoring system of one point for a successful Panenka that finishes in the back goal and five points if it goes in the goal without bouncing first.

THE CONTENT

CREATIVE GAMES

Small-sided games with a scoreboard, used to embrace fun and creativity.

CREATIVE GAME 1: CONNECT FOUR

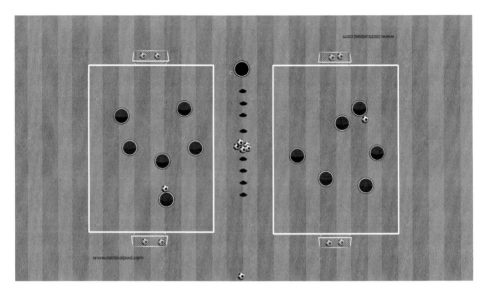

Figure 31. When a player scores a goal or is rewarded for positive behavior, they rush to the scoreboard to place a ball on top of one of their team's cones.

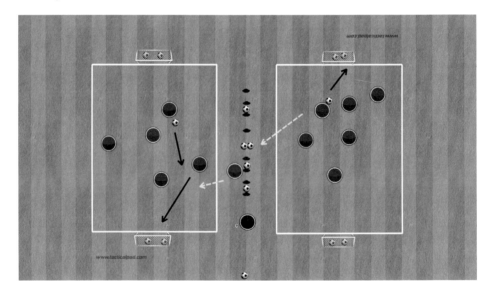

Figure 32. A fun and competitive progression is to allow the players to choose whether they add a ball to their team's scoreboard or remove one from the other team's scoreboard.

SCOREBOARD GAME—CONNECT FOUR

When a player scores a goal, the conceding team collects the ball and immediately continues the game while the goal scorer quickly goes to the scoreboard. Remember to occasionally send players who demonstrate positive play or model behavior to the scoreboard, to promote and praise these attributes.

The scoreboard in this game consists of four blue cones and four red cones, with a supply of balls nearby. The blue cones represent the blue scoreboard, and the red cones represent the red scoreboard. After a player scores or the coach instructs a player to go to the scoreboard due to positive play, they rush over and put a ball on their team's colored cones. The first set of teams to fill all four of their cones wins. This game involves collaboration between the teams wearing the same-colored bib, and players work hard because they know factors on the other pitch might result in them losing the game. When a team fills all four cones, they win the game. At that point, you may choose to reset the scoreboard and add the fun progression that the goal scorer or praised player can either put a ball on one of their team's cones or kick one off the other team's cone.

As always, be sure to let players know that you won't reward just goal scoring but also positive behaviors. Rewarding such behaviors will motivate players to repeat them. Scoreboard Soccer is designed to help in the holistic development of young people through praising and promoting characteristics such as teamwork, sportsmanship, and respect.

- Frequently varying the following four elements from session to session can help accommodate the number of players you have at your session and can also combat monotony.

- Modify the number of players.

- Vary whether teams play with a goalkeeper.

- Vary the size or number of goals used.

- Vary whether you run one game or multiple small-sided games simultaneously.

The following are other ways you can vary games from session to session:

- Vary the length or width of the pitch to give the players different problems and challenges.

- Introduce more cones to fill if you wish to prolong games.

- Progress by allowing players to add a point to their scoreboard or take one away from the opposition instead.

- Promote player autonomy by choosing captains who can praise players on the opposing team by sending them to the scoreboard.

CREATIVE GAME 2: CROSSBAR CHALLENGE

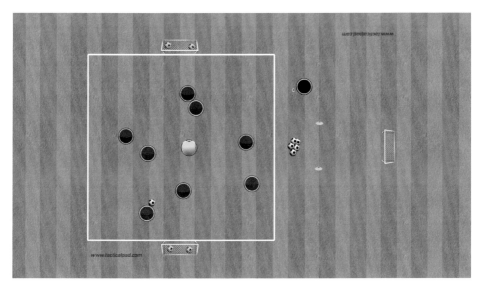

Figure 33. The goal scorer or rewarded player attempts to hit the crossbar with their shot.

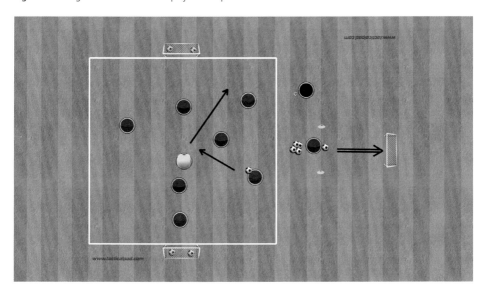

Figure 34. Designing and implementing fun scoreboards will motivate players to display maximum effort in the games in an attempt to be praised by their coach.

SCOREBOARD GAME—CROSSBAR CHALLENGE

When a player scores a goal, the conceding team immediately continues the game while the goal scorer quickly goes to the scoreboard.

This game consists of a simple scoreboard that the players always enjoy. Using a ball from the pile, the player lines up a shot at the crossbar from between the two yellow markers. If they hit the crossbar, a goal is added to their team's score in the game. Play for a set amount of time or to a set number of goals.

As with all scoreboards, the rewarded player should try to get a point via the scoreboard as quickly as possible so they can get back on the pitch to help their teammates, who are currently playing a player short, which increases the opposition's chance of scoring a goal or demonstrating positive play to be sent to the scoreboard. The playmaker (in figs. 33 and 34, in yello) is optional.

VARIATIONS

- Frequently varying the following four elements from session to session can help accommodate the number of players you have at your session and can also combat monotony.

- Modify the number of players.

- Vary whether teams play with a goalkeeper.

- Vary the size or number of goals used.

- Vary whether you run one game or multiple small-sided games simultaneously.

The following are other ways you can vary games from session to session:

- Vary the length or width of the pitch to give the players different problems and challenges.

- Increase or decrease the distance players need to try to hit the crossbar from.

- Allow players to punt the ball from their hands or utilize a bounce if they're finding it difficult to reach the crossbar.

CREATIVE GAME 3: SNAKES AND LADDERS

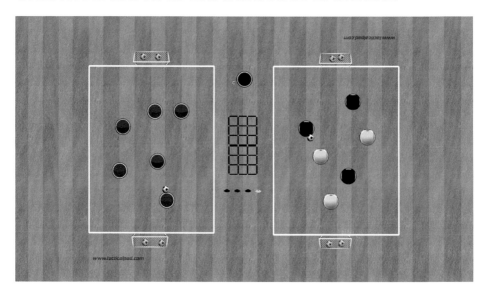

Figure 35. Classic board games can act as a scoreboard for young players.

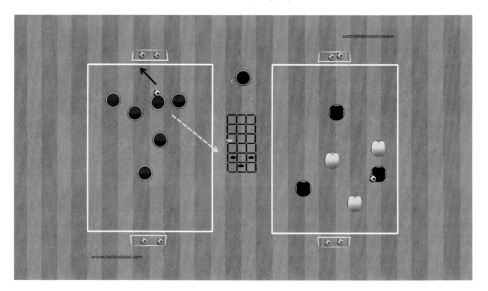

Figure 36. When players run to the scoreboard to roll for their team, those players still on the pitch need extra concentration to stay focused on the pitch and not on what their teammate rolled.

SCOREBOARD GAME—SNAKES AND LADDERS

When a player scores a goal, the conceding team collects the ball and immediately continues the game while the goal scorer quickly goes to the scoreboard. Remember to occasionally send players who demonstrate positive play or model behavior to the scoreboard, to promote and praise these attributes.

I've used many classic games and board games as scoreboards, and young players have always responded really well. Snakes and Ladders is one of their favorites, and they always ask for it. I find that they're desperate to make a good pass, score a goal, or praise teammates so the coach will praise them by allowing them to have a shot on the game board. In this game, four teams play (in figs. 35 and 36, red, blue, white, and black). This involves having four markers on the game board, and players roll the dice when they're at the scoreboard and move their team's marker up the board, progressing quicker when they reach a ladder and moving backward when they land on a snake. The game is fun and a good test of the concentration of those on the pitch, who are always shouting over to ask what number their teammate rolled or if they landed on a snake or a ladder. But they need to, of course, concentrate to prevent the other team from scoring and progressing up the board themselves!

As always, be sure to let players know that you won't reward just goal scoring but also positive behaviors. Rewarding such behaviors will motivate players to repeat them. Scoreboard Soccer is designed to help in the holistic development of young people through praising and promoting characteristics such as teamwork, sportsmanship, and respect.

VARIATIONS

- Frequently varying the following four elements from session to session can help accommodate the number of players you have at your session and can also combat monotony.

- Modify the number of players.

- Vary whether teams play with a goalkeeper.

- Vary the size or number of goals used.

- Vary whether you run one game or multiple small-sided games simultaneously.

The following are other ways you can vary games from session to session:

- Vary the length or width of the pitch to give the players different problems and challenges.

- Allow players to roll again if they throw the same number on both dice.

- Try other board games as scoreboards, letting the kids pick their favorites.

CREATIVE GAME 4: *Xs* AND *Os*

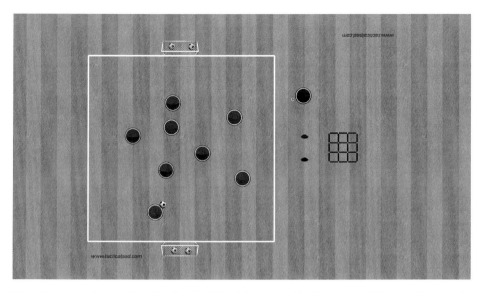

Figure 37. Set up a tic-tac-toe board on the side of the pitch. Players add a bib or a cone of their team's color to the board in an attempt to get three in a row.

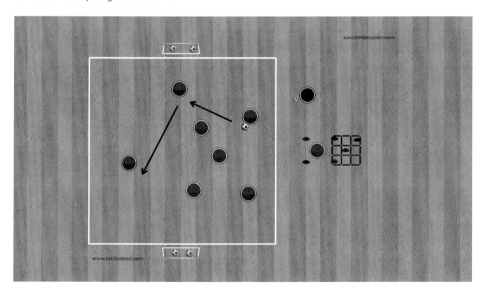

Figure 38. When a player comes off the pitch for scoring a goal or being praised for positive behavior, the player adds a bib or cone of their team's color to the board in an attempt to get three in a row.

SCOREBOARD GAME—Xs AND Os

When a player scores a goal, the conceding team collects a ball from the side of the pitch and immediately continues the game while the goal scorer quickly goes to the scoreboard.

A game you may know as Xs and Os or tic-tac-toe is the scoreboard in this game. When a player scores a goal or is sent to the scoreboard for positive behavior, the player adds a bib or a cone of their team's color to the matrix. The first team to get three in a row wins. If the game ends in a stalemate, the next player at the scoreboard can simply remove from the matrix a bib or cone belonging to the opposition. Continue in this fashion until a team wins.

As with all scoreboards, the rewarded player should try to get a point via the scoreboard as quickly as possible to get back on the pitch to help their team, which is currently playing a player short. This, of course, increases the opposition's chance of scoring a goal or demonstrating positive play and being sent to the scoreboard.

VARIATIONS

- Frequently varying the following four elements from session to session can help accommodate the number of players you have at your session and can also combat monotony.

- Modify the number of players.

- Vary whether teams play with a goalkeeper.

- Vary the size or number of goals used

- Vary whether you run one game or multiple small-sided games simultaneously.

The following are other ways you can vary games from session to session:

- Vary the length or width of the pitch to give the players different problems and challenges.

- Increase or decrease the distance between the pitch and the tic-tac-toe board, as you may want to use it for some disguised fitness or stamina work.

CREATIVE GAME 5: FIND NEMO

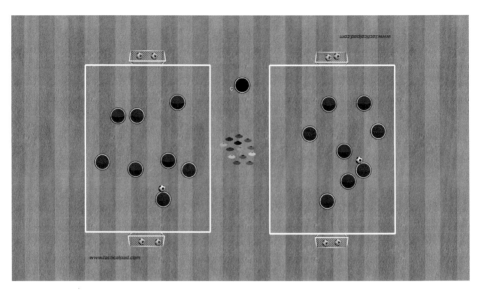

Figure 39. This scoreboard is setup using a variety of cones of different colors. When a player leaves the pitch, they get to look under one cone to try to find "Nemo."

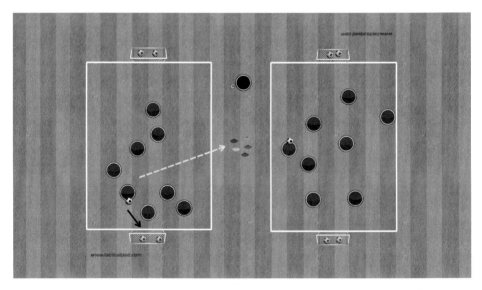

Figure 40. As players turn over cones that don't have Nemo under them, those cones go away, leaving fewer cones.

SCOREBOARD GAME—FIND NEMO

When a player scores a goal, the conceding team collects the ball and immediately continues the game while the goal scorer quickly goes to the scoreboard. Remember to send goal scorers not just to the scoreboard—throughout the game, if a player demonstrates positive play or behavior, you can reward this by saying "Well done" and sending them to the scoreboard too.

This fun scoreboard works well for all ages. For younger players, you may want to reference the film, *Finding Nemo*. For older ones, simply explain the game and let them learn through playing. Create the Great Barrier Reef by using a variety of different-color cones and explain to the players that while they're playing the games you'll hide Nemo under a cone (you might use a coin or do what I do—I use a small Nemo keyring). Use the scoreboard to reward goal scoring and praise effort, skill, attitude, and sportsmanship, by letting players flip a coin to see if they can find Nemo. The first team to find Nemo wins. So the more players score, work hard, and display a good attitude, the more the coach will send them to the scoreboard, and the greater the chance they'll have at finding Nemo and winning the game for their team. Once a team finds Nemo, reset the scoreboard and play again. This gives you a good opportunity to mix up the teams or rotate opponents if you have multiple pitches running.

Creating a big island of cones and surrounding it with two, three, or four games is a fun session, and I've found this game in particular to really motivate players to work hard and work together, as they know that only one team out of the four, six, or eight teams playing small-sided games can win, and they all want to be the player who finds the coin (or keyring).

VARIATIONS

- Frequently varying the following four elements from session to session can help accommodate the number of players you have at your session and can also combat monotony.

- Modify the number of players.

- Vary whether teams play with a goalkeeper.

- Vary the size or number of goals used.

- Vary whether you run one game or multiple small-sided games simultaneously.

The following are other ways you can vary games from session to session:

- Vary the length or width of the pitch to give the players different problems and challenges.

- Players have only five or six seconds to come and look under a cone. Don't allow any peeking!

- Progress the game by telling the players that they don't need to put the cone back if Nemo isn't underneath—they can just throw it off to the side! This generates more excitement as the supply of cones diminishes.

CREATIVE GAME 6: COCONUT SHY

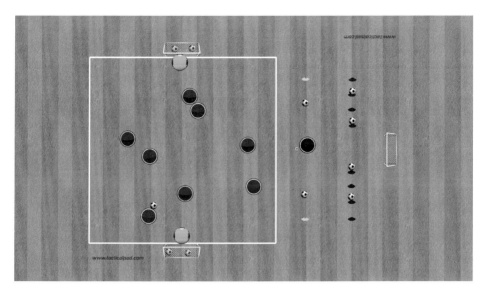

Figure 41. A player coming to the scoreboard has one attempt to pass a ball and knock another ball off a cone.

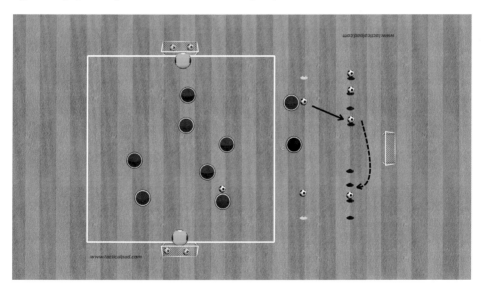

Figure 42. If successful at knocking a ball off a cone, the player adds that knocked-off ball to one of the other team's cones.

SCOREBOARD GAME—COCONUT SHY

When a player scores a goal, the conceding team collects the ball and immediately continues the game while the goal scorer quickly goes to the scoreboard to attempt a goal for their team through completing the Coconut Shy challenge.

Each team has a set of four cones. A ball sits on top of two of each team's cones. The aim is for the players to empty their team's four cones and fill the other team's; the first to do so wins. From a distance appropriate for the age and stage of players you're working with, the rewarded player comes to the scoreboard and gets one pass to try to knock a ball off their team's cones. If successful, they add this ball to the other team's cones. If unsuccessful, they put the ball they passed back and rejoin the game.

As with all scoreboards, the rewarded player should try to get a point via the scoreboard as quickly as possible to get back on the pitch to help their teammates, who are currently playing a player short. This increases the opposition's chance of scoring a goal or demonstrating positive play to be sent to the scoreboard.

- You can modify the following two elements depending on how many players you have and the age and stage of the group:

- Modify the number of players.

- Vary the size of goals used.

- Vary whether teams play with a goalkeeper.

- Vary whether you run one game or multiple small-sided games simultaneously.

The following are other ways you can vary games from session to session:

- Vary the length or width of the pitch to give the players different problems and challenges.

- Increase the number of cones and the number of balls the players need to knock off to prolong the game.

- Increase or decrease the length of the pass players need to knock a ball off the cone.

CREATIVE GAME 7: BANANAS VS. STRAWBERRIES

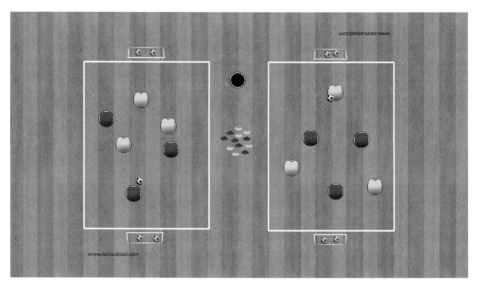

Figure 43. Set up the scoreboard by stacking several sets of two cones—one red and one yellow. Half of the stacks should have red on top, and half should have yellow on top.

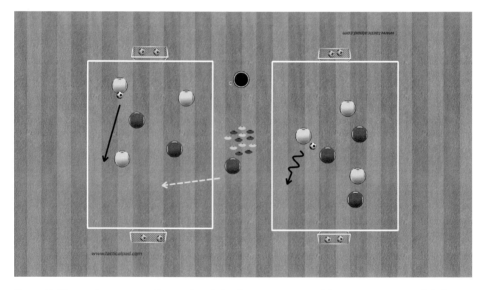

Figure 44. When a player comes to the scoreboard, they have a set amount of time to move as many of the bottom cones of their team's color to the top.

SCOREBOARD GAME—BANANAS VS. STRAWBERRIES

When a player scores a goal, the conceding team collects the ball and immediately continues the game while the goal scorer quickly goes to the scoreboard.

The scoreboard in this game consists of red and yellow cones. With younger players, I call this "Bananas vs. Strawberries," but with older players, I sometimes call it Brazil vs. Spain or let the players pick the names of the teams. In the middle of the pitches shown in figures 43 and 44, there are red cones with yellow cones underneath and yellow cones with red cones underneath. Ensure that there's an even spread of each color among the top cones. Players rewarded in the small-sided games come over and try to move the cones matching their team's color to the top. Players move one cone at a time when the come to the scoreboard before returning to the game. After a set time limit, call an end to the game and bring the players over to count which team got the most cones on top. Was it the strawberries (red cones) or the bananas (yellow cones)?

These teamwork games are great, and it can be nice to see players embrace each other at the end of games. Instead of having six yellows versus six reds, having them split into two teams of three increases involvement and touches, but they're still working together to win the game. Scoreboard Soccer, though, is more than just winning as it is ultimately about the process that leads to success. That can be things like encouraging teammates and never giving up. Games set up in this fashion give a great opportunity for fun competition, and you can mix up the red and yellow teammates between each game to keep that competition alive but allow players to interact and work with a variety of different individuals.

VARIATIONS

- Frequently varying the following four elements from session to session can help accommodate the number of players you have at your session and can also combat monotony.

- Modify the number of players.

- Vary whether teams play with a goalkeeper.

- Vary the size or number of goals used.

- Vary whether you run one game or multiple small-sided games simultaneously.

The following are other ways you can vary games from session to session:

- Vary the length or width of the pitch to give the players different problems and challenges.

- Involve players more by letting them pick the names of the teams, set the time limit, and pick their own teams after each round.

- Increase the distance a player needs to run to the scoreboard, to promote some fun fitness work, perhaps even requiring ladders or hurdles on their way to the scoreboard. This will also delay the player returning and give the opposition a longer overload to deal with and the other team a bigger challenge of defending outnumbered.

CREATIVE GAME 8: EGG AND SPOON

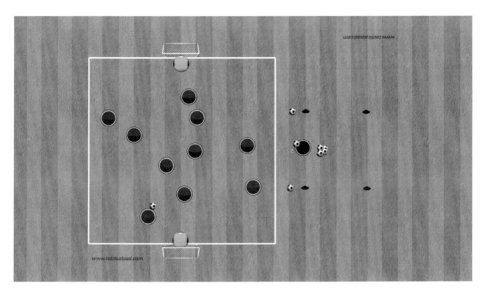

Figure 45. The scoreboard consists of a pair of cones for each team, eggs, and spoons.

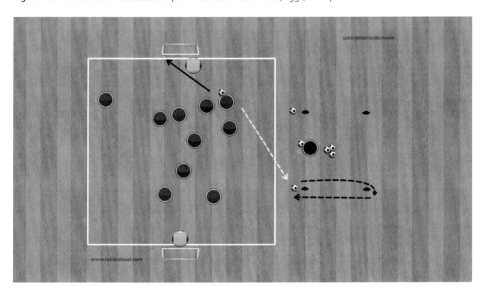

Figure 46. The rewarded player attempts to carry an egg on a spoon while either running to and around a cone and back or while dribbling a ball to and around a cone and back.

SCOREBOARD GAME—EGG AND SPOON

When a player scores a goal, the coach passes in a new ball, and the teams immediately continue the game while the goal scorer quickly goes to the scoreboard.

Younger players love the egg-and-spoon race, and they love soccer, so combined, this makes for a fun, competitive game with lots of hidden learning. The player who scores or demonstrates positive play is rewarded by getting to go to the scoreboard, place an egg on a spoon, and run to and around a cone and back without dropping the egg. If they do, it's a point for their team, and they quickly rejoin the game. If they drop the egg, they put it back at the start with the spoon and quickly rejoin the game with no additional point scored. Although fun and a good way to create overloads and underloads on the pitch that last a bit longer, to enhance problem solving, the scoreboard is also great for getting younger players to work on crucial motor skills, like balance, coordination, and concentration.

Older players love this game, too. I really enjoy playing this one!

- Frequently varying the following four elements from session to session can help accommodate the number of players you have at your session and can also combat monotony.

- Modify the number of players.

- Vary whether teams play with a goalkeeper.

- Vary the size or number of goals used.

- Vary whether you run one game or multiple small-sided games simultaneously.

The following are other ways you can vary games from session to session:

- Vary the length or width of the pitch to give the players different problems and challenges.

- Progress the game by challenging players to not only balance the egg on the spoon and go around the cone but also to do it with a ball at their feet. It adds another layer of fun but is great for players to work on small touches, concentration, and lifting their head as they travel with the ball.

CREATIVE GAME 9: VOLCANOES VS. SPACESHIPS

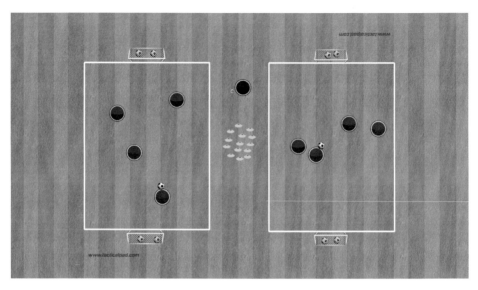

Figure 47. The team with the most cones—spaceships or volcanoes—wins.

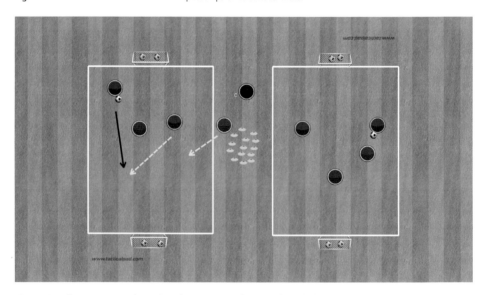

Figure 48. In between games, have the volcanoes teams, for example, switch pitches.

SCOREBOARD GAME—VOLCANOES VS. SPACESHIPS

When a player scores a goal, the conceding team collects the ball and immediately continues the game while the goal scorer quickly goes to the scoreboard.

The red teams on each pitch play as volcanoes, while the blue teams on each pitch play as spaceships. Half of the cones in the middle start upside down (spaceships) while the other half start the right side up (volcanoes). Play the small-sided games for a set amount of time. Each team's aim is to collect as many cones representing the team as possible. So if, for example, a blue-team player scores, they quickly run to the scoreboard and turn a "volcano" (right side up) cone upside down and return to the pitch. The team with the most cones—spaceships or volcanoes—after the set time limit wins the game, and you can reset the scoreboard and play again. After each game, you may want to rotate teams. For example, in figure 48, the spaceships on each pitch can swap over to play the other team of volcanoes.

I've shown this game in figures 47 and 48 with smaller numbers. The scoreboard is a great way to create 1v2 and 2v1 situations on the pitch to support the development of decision-making within these scenarios. But the game can work just as well with more players.

VARIATIONS

- Frequently varying the following four elements from session to session can help accommodate the number of players you have at your session and can also combat monotony.

- Modify the number of players.

- Vary whether teams play with a goalkeeper.

- Vary the size or number of goals used.

- Vary whether you run one game or multiple small-sided games simultaneously.

The following are other ways you can vary games from session to session:

- Vary the length or width of the pitch to give the players different problems and challenges.

- Don't tell players how long the games are, and set a timer that goes off when the game is over. This can generate a lot of energy for players to get to the scoreboard as often as possible. The players get excited when the game is over and run to the scoreboard to see who won.

- I've shown other games with one pitch running, and I show this one (see fig. 47 and fig. 48) with two pitches running, but you could have four pitches running, with all the cones in the middle of the four. Four teams would represent the spaceships, and the other four would represent the volcanoes. After each round, you could rotate the teams around to play different oppositions, but the theme of volcanoes vs. spaceships would remain. You can even do a mini tournament, three points for a win, one for a draw, and zero for a loss. Every team would play each other once or twice and accumulate the scores for the spaceships and the volcanoes throughout the session.

- For older players, you may not want to call it volcanoes vs. spaceships but simply use it as a good tool to work on overloads, underloads, and recovery runs.

CREATIVE GAME 10: INDIANA JONES

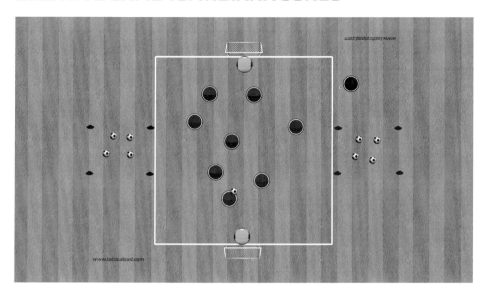

Figure 49. Each team has their own scoreboard. The winner is the team that has the most balls in their scoreboard at the end of the game.

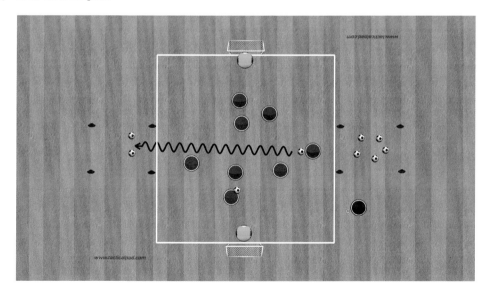

Figure 50. The rewarded player takes a ball from the opposition's scoreboard and dribbles it across the pitch, through the live game, to deliver the ball to their team's scoreboard.

SCOREBOARD GAME—INDIANA JONES

When a player scores a goal, the conceding team collects the ball and immediately continues the game while the goal scorer quickly goes to the scoreboard.

This game has two scoreboards, one for each team, and the aim is for each team to have more balls in their scoreboard by the end of the game, or you can play so that it's the first to get all the balls wins. Figure 49 shows that the goal scorer or praised player takes a ball from the other team's scoreboard and dribbles across the pitch to put it in their team's. As with all scoreboard games, the game is always live; therefore, the challenge here is for the player to be able to dribble through a live game to get their team a point. This is a great scoreboard to encourage and embrace dribbling the ball, and therefore, that may be something to reward during the game.

This scoreboard also challenges players in the game regarding scanning and awareness, looking out for players dribbling across the pitch as the game is played. Be sure that you deliver this with the health and safety of your players in mind. If you suspect that the players aren't controlled and sensible enough for this environment, don't use this game, or add a condition that the ball must stay below waist height during the game.

- Frequently varying the following four elements from session to session can help accommodate the number of players you have at your session and can also combat monotony.

- Modify the number of players.

- Vary whether teams play with a goalkeeper.

- Vary the size or number of goals used.

- Vary whether you run one game or multiple small-sided games simultaneously.

The following are other ways you can vary games from session to session:

- Vary the length or width of the pitch to give the players different problems and challenges.

- Increase the distance between scoreboards to ensure even more running with the ball.

- Again, always be sure to know the maturity and ability of your players and use scoreboard games with players of appropriate age and stage to ensure that games are played safely.

CREATIVE GAME 11: SPLAT ATTACK

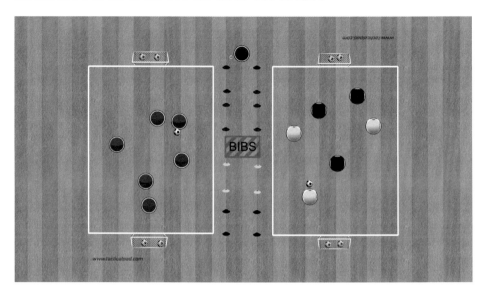

Figure 51. This scoreboard consists of four individual scoreboards. Players grab bibs from the central pile to score for their team.

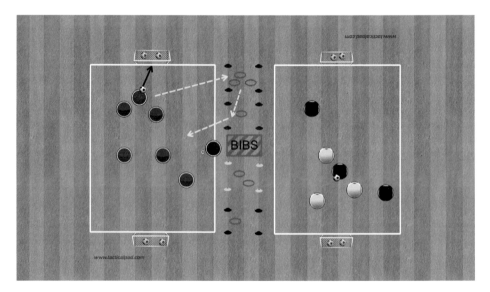

Figure 52. Once players have exhausted the central pile of bibs, they can add points to their scoreboard by removing a bib from an opposing team's scoreboard.

SCOREBOARD GAME—SPLAT ATTACK

When a player scores a goal, the conceding team collects the ball and immediately continues the game while the goal scorer quickly goes to the scoreboard.

The scoreboard in this game consists of four five-by-five-yard boxes that act as each team's scoreboard. Place a pile of bibs in between the active pitches. When a team scores a goal, the scorer runs over, grabs a bib, and throws it into their team's scoreboard. The team with the most bibs in their scoreboard after a set time limit wins. Progress to letting players steal bibs from the other team's scoreboard once all bibs are gone from the central pile. This game can easily be adapted to use only two central scoreboards (for example, two red and two blue teams could share a red scoreboard and blue scoreboard); however, figures 51 and 52 show how scoreboards can work with four or more teams, and this idea may be transferable to other scoreboards too. It's always good to try what works and learn or develop new games and concepts.

Be sure to let players know you won't reward just goal scoring but also positive behaviors, such as ingenuity and leadership, by sending them to the scoreboard. Rewarding such behaviors will motivate players to repeat them.

VARIATIONS

- Frequently varying the following four elements from session to session can help accommodate the number of players you have at your session and can also combat monotony.

- Modify the number of players.

- Vary whether teams play with a goalkeeper.

- Vary the size or number of goals used.

- Vary whether you run one game or multiple small-sided games simultaneously.

The following are other ways you can vary games from session to session:

- Vary the length or width of the pitch to give the players different problems and challenges.

- Instead of four teams, you could do this with two teams, with a red and a blue team on each pitch and two central scoreboards (one red, one blue) instead of four.

- If you have enough balls, players can use balls instead of bibs to place points in the scoreboard. This gives players even more touches as they steal balls from the other team's scoreboards, turn, dribble, and stop it in theirs.

CREATIVE GAME 12: SNOWMAN

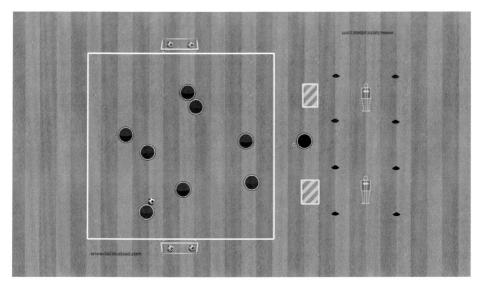

Figure 53. This scoreboard is set up with two mannequins, one for each team, and a pile of clothes to dress the team's mannequin in.

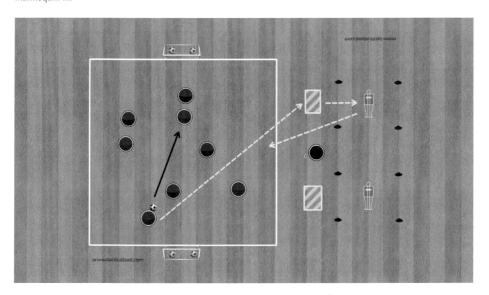

Figure 54. Players add one piece of clothing to their team's mannequin each time they're sent to the scoreboard.

SCOREBOARD GAME—SNOWMAN

When a player scores a goal, the conceding team collects the ball and immediately continues the game while the goal scorer quickly goes to the scoreboard. Remember to occasionally send players who demonstrate positive play or model behavior to the scoreboard, to promote and praise these attributes.

This is a fun game to use at near the winter holidays. Each team has a mannequin in their scoreboard and a pile of clothes. You can determine the clothes for your game, but I've used a jersey, a bib, a hat, sunglasses, a scarf, and a ball—to go at the mannequin's feet. On scoring a goal or being praised by the coach, a player runs over and puts one item on their team's snowman (mannequin). The first team to completely dress the snowman wins.

As always, be sure to let players know that you won't reward just goal scoring but also positive behaviors. Rewarding such behaviors will motivate players to repeat them. Scoreboard Soccer is designed to help in the holistic development of young people through praising and promoting characteristics such as teamwork, sportsmanship, and respect.

- Frequently varying the following four elements from session to session can help accommodate the number of players you have at your session and can also combat monotony.

- Modify the number of players.

- Vary whether teams play with a goalkeeper.

- Vary the size or number of goals used.

- Vary whether you run one game or multiple small-sided games simultaneously.

The following are other ways you can vary games from session to session:

- Vary the length or width of the pitch to give the players different problems and challenges.

- If you don't want to use the winter theme, you might call the game "Hangman," where the aim is to dress the other team's mannequin.

- Allow the players to name the game or the mannequins. Perhaps after their favorite professional players.

THE COACHING

COACHING AND SCOREBOARD SOCCER

The Scoreboard Soccer concept and content allow for many coachable moments, which are highlighted in this section.

THE COACHING—INDIVIDUAL TECHNIQUE

Scoreboard Soccer games are designed to grant players the freedom to practice and problem solve. As coaches, we should resist the temptation to give answers and solve problems for players, as this takes away their ownership of learning. This is crucial for the evolution of the player and the sport itself. Sometimes we need to apply skillful silence, not telling the players how the game should be played but leaving them to discover how the game could be played. And, of course, sometimes we need to give hints, tips, and direction to help players with the development of their individual techniques and understanding of the game. I find that it's important to find the balance and that some players need more help than others, which is why it's crucial to give space for observation and identify which players are actively problem solving certain techniques and taking ownership of their learning and which players need help and guidance—as opposed to what I call a blanket approach to coaching. I equate a blanket approach to coaching with soccer stereotyping, planning sessions with the belief that everyone within those sessions needs to hear and be taught the same thing. An example of this would be a coach delivering a session for fifteen nine-year-olds, having already predetermined that the coach will teach all of the players to pass the ball with the inside of the foot, aim with the standing foot, and hit the center of the ball. Will players who are already competent at this skill take anything from this session? Or will the session possibly be counterproductive for them?

Scoreboard Soccer allows coaches to meet players where they are on their journey. You aren't creating a session for fifteen players; you're creating a session for individuals (James, Daniel, Tyler, Connor, etc.). During the small-sided games, coaches can fill the environment with praise and encouragement but also use tools such as skillful silence and comprehensive observation to identify the individual needs of players. Once the coach identifies these needs, the coach can implement individual coaching. There are many ways to do this during Scoreboard Soccer games:

- Call individual players to the side and offer individual coaching points or advice while the rest of the players continue to play.

- Use the scoreboard to teach the technique needed for success. If it's a passing scoreboard, for example, spend some time working on the player's passing technique while they're at the scoreboard.

- Coach within the games. For example, if a player is consistently making similar mistakes, you might freeze the game after they make a mistake and recreate the situation, giving the player some guidance and coaching points. Asking players questions can be a great way to engage them in the learning process.

- Plan practices before or after scoreboard games to develop technical proficiency.

THE COACHING—ATTACKING SCENARIOS

Scoreboard Soccer games give players a lot of freedom to create, problem solve, and express themselves, but it can also give coaches an opportunity to coach crucial fundamentals in situations, such as 3v3, 4v4, and 5v5, that occur constantly in 11v11. When a team has the ball in these situations, the players should look to spread out to create as much space on the pitch as possible. In a 3v3, for example, players can spread out as much as possible and create three 1v1 situations all over the pitch. The space created by spreading out also allows for movements into new areas of the pitch for receiving or running to the ball and the opportunity for a lot of rotation between players.

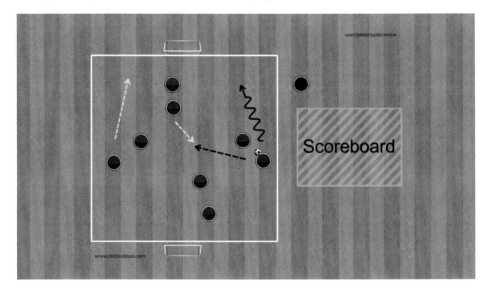

Figure 55. Attacking balanced: providing length, width, depth, and rotations create space and smaller matchups that occur within 11v11 games

KEY COACHING POINTS

- Provide length: Players look to stretch the opposition by going as far up the pitch as possible. This can give teams forward passes and create space for other players to move into and receive the ball.

- Provide width: Look to have options as wide as possible. Getting the ball into these areas can pull the opposition away from the central area and the goal they're trying to defend and open up forward passing lanes.

- Provide depth: Players who provide depth can help with ball circulation and attracting the opposition up the pitch and away from the space or goal they're defending. Depth is provided by a player dropping off the game a little and giving an option for the team to go back and maybe restart attacks or control the tempo of the game for a while. This option is great for switching play when, for example, the team isn't having much success down the right and passing back to the player providing depth can maybe switch it to the left or fake to switch and play forward. Players providing depth can also be crucial in slowing down opposition counterattacks.

- Work in rotations: As a group, players should look to rotate the roles and be unpredictable but organized at the same time.

The Scoreboard Soccer concept is designed to challenge players with constant overloads and underloads. This creates many 3v2, 4v3, and 5v4 situations. When a team has the ball in these situations, players should look to spread out and make the pitch as big as possible and combine this with quick, decisive play. Encourage players to make the most of the attacking overload and stress that these situations won't last long, as the player at the scoreboard will be recovering back on the pitch to help their team as quickly as possible.

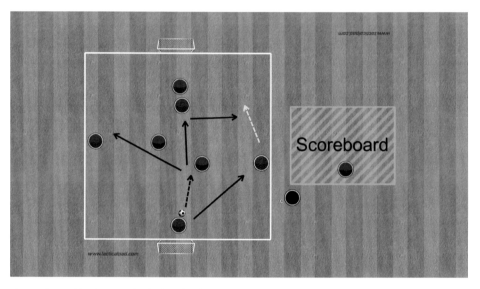

Figure 56. Attacking in an overload: when there's an overload due to the opposition having a player at the scoreboard, quick play, penetration, and balance help the team with the overload to make the most of this situation.

- Play quick: Create width and length quickly to open up passing lanes and space to run into with or without the ball.

- Penetrate: Cause problems for the opposition by offering some form of penetration—for example, taking players on and looking to use the extra player as a decoy by pretending to pass before dribbling by a defender. Other ways to penetrate include making penetrating runs, such as overlaps, underlaps, and runs in behind the defense, or making penetrating passes, such as through balls, passes over the top, and disguised revere passes.

- Balance: Stay organized by ensuring that not all players look to penetrate, which may take space away from teammates. It may be that a player provides balance to the team by staying back to ensure that teams aren't caught on the counterattack, or if teammates are unable to penetrate, you may need to pass back to this player to build another attack. This player may also be useful for tracking the movement of the player returning from the scoreboard, either by communicating with their teammates that the player is approaching or ensuring that the player can't be easily passed to on a turnover of possession.

During the games, it'll frequently be the case that the team in possession has a player at the scoreboard, especially if you stipulate that the scoring team gets to start with the ball. This will create 2v3, 3v4, or 4v5 situations, further creating opportunities for players to practice taking on one, two, or maybe even three players themselves. This is a difficult skill and will likely result in a lot of failure, but as coaches, we must embrace this. The more players attempt, fail, and try again, the more they'll improve through trial and error. These situations can also help players work on shielding and protecting the ball as well as movement off the ball, as players will need to work hard to lose opposition players and find space to receive the ball.

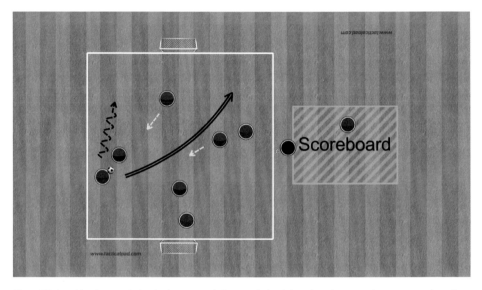

Figure 57. Attacking in an underload: when a team is in an underload situation, players work to remove a player from the equation, protect the ball, and commit defenders.

KEY COACHING POINTS

- Take someone on: As a player with the ball in an outnumbered situation, can you quickly look to take the ball past a player and remove them from the equation? This quickly creates a balanced scenario for your team.

- Protect the ball: Every situation is different, and scanning and awareness are crucial. It may be the best option to hold on to the ball to wait for another player on your team to join the attack (the player returning from the scoreboard, for example).

- Commit defenders: A great skill for a player to possess is close control that can commit more than one player to the ball. Can the person on the ball look to commit two players to the ball through their close control and direction of travel, then shift the ball quickly to play through or around these players to a teammate? This gives a team a numbers advantage going forward.

THE COACHING—DEFENDING SCENARIOS

Scoreboard Soccer games give players a lot of freedom to create, problem solve, and express themselves, but the games also give coaches an opportunity to coach crucial fundamentals in situations such as 3v3, 4v4, and 5v5—situations that occur constantly in 11v11 games. When their team doesn't have the ball in these situations, players should look to get compact and deny the opposition as much space on the pitch as possible. In a 3v3, for example, players can get close together and hunt the ball in packs, never giving the opposition 1v1 situations to exploit. This denies the opposition space and hopefully forces them back or out wide and away from the goal the defending team is protecting. The longer the defenders can force the opposition into playing this way, the more chances of a mistake increase—such as forcing a forward pass that's intercepted or goes out of play or a player taking a heavy touch of the ball that can lead to a turnover of possession.

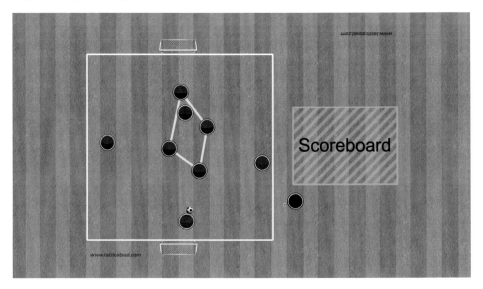

Figure 58. Defending balanced: a team in a defensive situation can work to defend balanced by denying, getting compact, covering, and communicating.

- Deny: Don't give the player on the ball any space or time. The player closest to the player on the ball should quickly deny them space and time by closing down the ball while their teammates move in conjunction to form a compact defensive unit.

- Compact: Close the spaces between players and move as a unit to put pressure on the ball, always scanning and being mindful of where the opposition's players move and not allowing any passes to be played through your compact unit.

- Cover: As the player in the compact unit closest to the opposition puts some pressure on the ball, the other players can provide cover so that if the attacker starts to dribble and gets past the defender closest to the ball another defender is close enough to engage the attacker.

- Communicate: As a defensive unit, you need to all be working together with the same game plan. Communication helps to ensure defensive security when it comes to who will put pressure on the ball and who will cover them. It also helps let other players know to get compact and move together. As a team, you may also have a plan to push the opposition into certain areas of the pitch, such as away from the goal or into areas where you're confident you can try to win the ball. Again, communication is crucial to applying these strategies.

During scoreboard games, it'll frequently be the case that the team out of possession will have an extra player on the pitch. This creates opportunities for players to practice pressing, being more aggressive in their approach to winning the ball back, and staying focused to ensure that they don't overcommit let the ball be played forward to the player returning from the scoreboard.

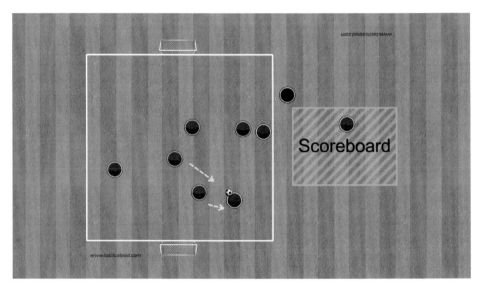

Figure 59. Defending in an overload: players in an overload can press, tackle, and work together to make the most of the temporary overload.

- Press: Can you make the most of the momentary numbers advantage by looking to win the ball back quickly and perhaps having more than one player going to try to win the ball back, making it difficult for the player in possession?

- Tackle: The closest defender who engages the ball may be able to take more risks and work on trying to tackle and win the ball. It's important to ensure that the extra teammate is providing cover in case the tackler is unsuccessful.

- Work together: If the team doesn't move as a unit, it will defeat the purpose of having an extra player. If the group becomes disjointed, it may mean the attacking team's players can pick off members of the team one by one and work their way through the defenders with dribbling skills and forward passes.

One of the most common scenarios in Scoreboard Soccer games that occur frequently in soccer is a team defending outnumbered, especially if as the scoring player goes to the scoreboard the conceding team restarts with the ball immediately. This gives the defenders an opportunity to work on the very realistic game scenario of having to slow down an attack in the hopes that their player will recover quickly from the scoreboard. The attackers will, of course, be making this difficult as they look to take quick advantage of their extra player.

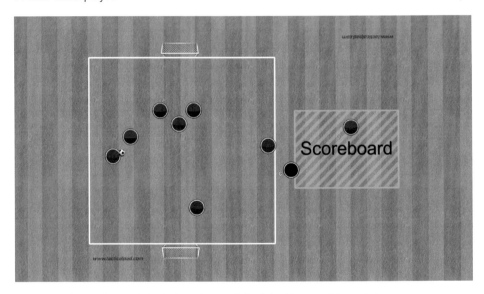

Figure 60. Defending in an underload: players in an underload should protect, delay, and show.

KEY COACHING POINTS

- Protect: It's important for players in an underload to always remember that they're protecting the goal. In small-sided play, the goal may signify a forward pass or a defense splitting through the ball. Regardless, players have the target where they don't want the opposition to go, so they should react quickly to drop back, get compact, and protect the goal and the middle of the pitch.

- Delay: As the outnumbered team without the ball, players in an underload look to slow down the attacking team and delay them so their player or players can get back and help. This can be done by putting pressure on the ball but not diving in to win the ball, just keeping their body between the ball and where the attacker wants to go while the defender's teammates provide cover nearby to deny as much space for the attacking team as possible.

- Show: When outnumbered, it can help to show the player on the ball where the defender wants them to go. This can be done by approaching in a manner that gives them a simple pass to their left, for example. But a covering teammate can see by their teammate's body language and approach that they're showing the opposing player to pass to their left and can then be quick to press that pass and pressure the receiving player in the hope of winning the ball. The approaching player may show the attacker away from all their teammates and show them toward the boundaries of the pitch. By channeling a player in this manner, a defending player can eliminate the numbers advantage and start to approach the situation as a 1v1.

THE COACHING—CONSTANT TRANSITIONS

Scoreboard Soccer is a games-based approach to coaching. Although this section gives the coach some fundamental ideas to help young players when they have the ball and when they don't, the majority of the time, players should be playing the game and learning on the job. Let the games be the teacher.

This chapter covers situations where the numbers on the pitch are even, such as 3v3 and 4v4, but also underloads and overloads, such as 2v1 or 3v4. The biggest challenge for players is the constant transitions between these moments, such as defending with three defenders against four attackers but winning the ball and suddenly playing as three attackers against four defenders. The scoreboard games give players constant transitions that they can attempt to react to and find success in, providing crucial learning by mistakes and evolving as players due to being constantly exposed to these situations.

As a coach, you may simply look to increase awareness and stress the importance of the attacking and defending principles outlined in this chapter and the crucial moments between the two, which we call transition.

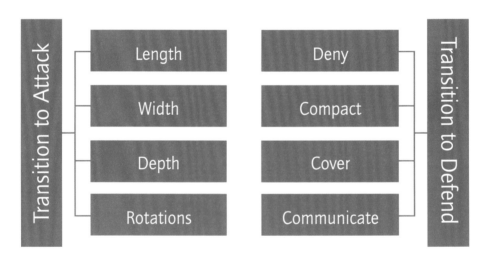

Figure 61. Transitions.

THE CURRICULUM

STORYBOOK SOCCER

A way to engage children in soccer through fun and imaginative story lines, maximizing the use of their motor skills while promoting confidence, creativity, and teamwork.

STORYBOOK SOCCER—INTRODUCTORY ACTIVITY

Unstructured and child-led play is a crucial part of youth development. It helps promote physical literacy and key motor skills. Interaction with other children also plays a crucial part in the development of social skills, such as communication and collaboration.

Regarding the Storybook Soccer curriculum that follows, I recommend building in frequent unstructured and child-led play. Let the children be children, and as a coach, be on hand to ensure that they're all safe and having fun within the environment. I tend to start most sessions in this curriculum with unstructured play, which I call "free play" for the players. At times, I also incorporate free play during or at the end of the session. I think it's a good coaching tool to, if you feel that the children are becoming disengaged or that your session component isn't working the way you'd like, break into free play for a short time before moving onto the next component.

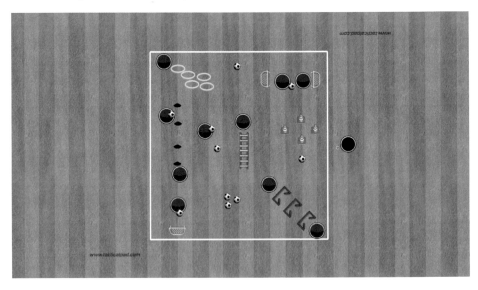

Figure 62. Storybook Soccer Introductory Activity.

CURRICULUM: Storybook Soccer

SESSION: 1

AGE: 4–12

STAGE: Love Football

THEMES: Fun, Coordination, Building a Relationship With the Ball, Pirates

COMPONENT 1: STEERING THE PIRATE SHIP

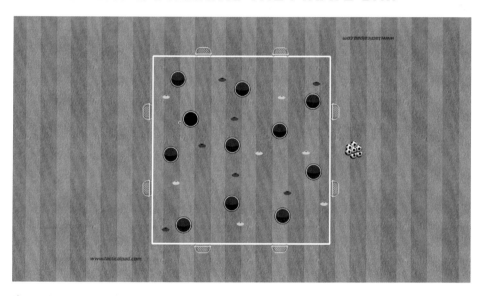

Figure 63. Scatter cones (red underneath yellow and yellow underneath red) and give each player a "pirate ship" (ball) to steer around the "sea" (pitch).

ENVIRONMENT

In an area appropriate for the number of players you're working with, have cones scattered all around the area, as shown in figure 63. Red cones should have a yellow cone underneath, and yellow cones should have a red cone underneath. Start by encouraging players to run around and jump over as many cones as they can. This serves as a simple activity to introduce young players to the area and equipment. Progress by giving each player a ball and enthusiastically explaining that the ball today will be their pirate ship! The pitch is the sea, and the cones are rocks. Say, "Let's sail our pirate ship around the sea and try not to crash!"

BEHAVIORS

Building relationships with young players is crucial. Focus more on whom you're coaching as opposed to what you're coaching them in. Learn their names, encourage high fives, praise their efforts, and be the coach you'd want if you were their age. Some players may not totally engage at first—they may be running around wildly or kicking or throwing balls all over the place. If that happens, I encourage you to ask yourself, Is this a bad thing? If you can see them and they're safe and being physically active, you may be able to let a lot slide. Spending energy trying to refocus such players may be to the detriment of the rest of the group. In my experience, if you focus on creating a really fun, engaging, and story-based environment for the majority of players, the disengaged ones will choose when to join in. But if you give them a lot of attention when they're doing what they shouldn't be doing, they may just keep doing it.

VARIATIONS

- Challenge players to demonstrate different jumping styles over the cones (legs together, hopping, star jumps, etc.).

- Ask players to sail their pirate ship by pretending their hands are on a big wheel that they need to turn to move the ship (the ball). This may help keep them from using their hands on the ball too much.

- Introduce fun commands for players to try when sailing their ship, such as *scrub the deck*, *climb the ladder*, and *walk the plank*—all represented by different touches on the ball.

- Some of the most fun and effective coaching sessions I've delivered for this age group have involved engaging the parents or guardians in the session. The children have yet to develop listening skills, but they'll try to copy the example set by positive role models in their lives.

COMPONENT 2: RUBIES AND GOLD

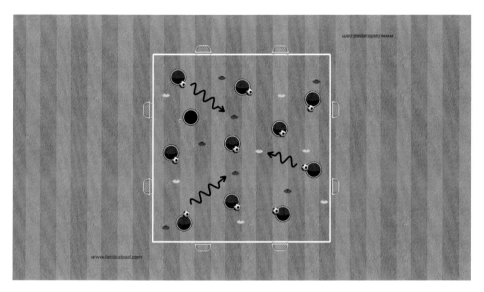

Figure 64. Players have a set amount of time to switch the top cone in as many cone stacks as they can.

ENVIRONMENT

You may ask players to leave their ball and initially start this race without the ball before progressing to taking the ball with them and dribble as best they can. Ask the players, "What do pirates love?" and congratulate anyone who says "treasure" or "gold." Tell them that you're going to see how much treasure they can collect. Give players thirty seconds to run around the area. Every time they flip a cone, they get a point. Since all cones are in stacks of two, if it's yellow on top, they need to flip it and put red on top and vice versa. Reference the red cones as red rubies and the yellow cones as gold, to stick to the pirate theme.

BEHAVIORS

With time and patience, over the course of a number of sessions, you should be able to start to encourage small, slow touches of the ball to manipulate it toward a cone—with behaviors like using the foot to stop the ball and then quick balance and coordination to bend over, flip the cone, and go again. Embrace the fun competition, asking players what their score was and challenging them to try to get more next time.

VARIATIONS

- Include parents or guardians in the session, to demonstrate positive examples for the players.

- Depending on the age and stage, you may split the group into two teams. One team tries to get all the red rubies on top, and the other tries to get all the yellow gold on top.

- Over time, implement foot skills, such as five touches of the ball before the player can flip a cone. Other coordination skills, such as bouncing the ball twice or throwing and catching before flipping a cone, are also great for children this age.

COMPONENT 3: PROGRESSION OF COMPONENT 2

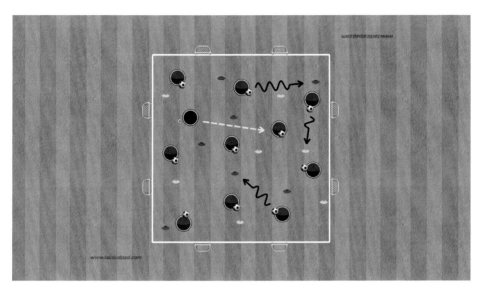

Figure 65. Players keep the ball from the shark.

ENVIRONMENT

Once players are having fun and are comfortable dribbling the ball around and flipping cones, progress the story and session by asking the players, "What might we find in the sea?" This is a great way to engage them in the session, and players will enjoy telling you about whales, octopi, and fish. In this progression, the coach becomes a shark who's trying to steal the players' treasure as they sail around the sea. The coach simply looks to chase players and get a touch of the player's pirate ship (ball). As you're in the sea, if players get caught by the shark, they need to do five starfish jumps before they can start dribbling again.

BEHAVIORS

This is a fun progression to the story, but with time, perhaps subconsciously, the players will be improving their skills. They think they're sailing a ship around the sea, looking for treasure and avoiding the shark; however, we know that they're dribbling a ball around a pitch, looking for cones and avoiding the defender.

VARIATIONS

- Include parents or guardians in the session, to demonstrate positive examples for the players.

- Depending on the age and stage of the players, you might allocate a player to become the shark.

- You might stipulate that when the shark gets the player's ball, the shark keeps it, and the player becomes the shark.

- Some players may be able to try to collect points during this exercise, and some may simply look to stay away from the shark. Both methods within the same activity are fine. At this age, some players will be able to do more than others.

COMPONENT 4: *X* MARKS THE SPOT

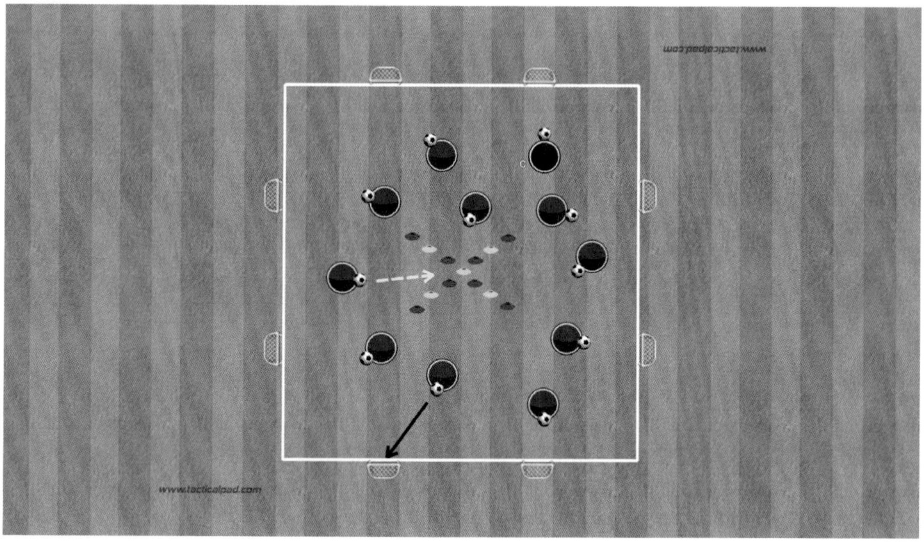

Figure 66. Once players score a goal, they run to the central *X* and flip a cone from red to yellow (or yellow to red) to score a point.

ENVIRONMENT

Using the cones from the previous components, create a large *X* in the middle of the area, still keeping cones in stacks—yellow cones on top of red and red cones on top of yellow. As you introduce the fun of kicking the ball in a goal, players try to get as many points as they can in this fun game. On the coach's command, players dribble to a goal, kick the ball in, pick the ball up with their hands, and run to the central *X*. By flipping a cone, they get a point, and then the process starts again. Essentially every time they score, they can go flip a cone to signal a point for themselves. Encourage players to count their score, and after a set time, ask them how many points they got.

SCOREBOARD SOCCER

BEHAVIORS

Introduce kicking the ball into the net as a fun and celebrated thing to do. If you don't have goals, you might use benches or cones. Or perhaps you'll need to adapt the activity by asking players to dribble to the outside line of the pitch before picking up the ball and running back to give themselves a point. Praise effort as opposed to outcome, so players know that effort is the important thing. For example, for a young player who normally uses their hands to throw the ball into the net but on this occasion tries to kick it, even if they miss the net, praise the effort and tell them it's great that they're trying to kick the ball and that they get two points for their great effort.

VARIATIONS

- Include parents or guardians in the session, to demonstrate positive examples for the players.

- Can anyone beat the coach? Play the game to give a good visual demonstration of what the players need to do. Also challenge them to beat your score.

- Depending on the age and stage of the players, you may play this game in two teams—the red team trying to get the rubies on top and the yellow team trying to get the gold on top. Play for a set time period, then ask the players to come in and count how many points each team achieved.

- You can easily adapt this setup by keeping the basics of the activity the same but changing the central activity. The Volcanoes vs. Spaceships, Find Nemo, and Splat Attack games earlier in this book provide good ideas for the central activity in this setup.

CURRICULUM: Storybook Soccer

SESSION: 2

AGE: 4–12

STAGE: Love Football

THEMES: Fun, Dribbling, Social Skills, Animals

COMPONENT 1: ANIMAL SOCCER

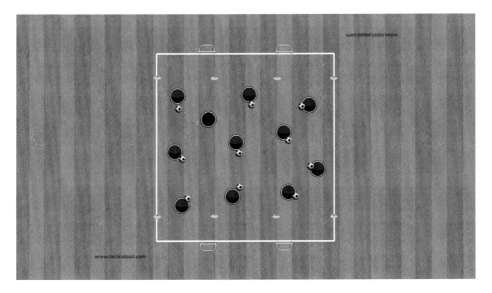

Figure 67. Players mimic animals to move around on the field.

ENVIRONMENT

I normally start this session with a fun tag-based game before asking the players to each get a ball for a game of animal soccer. I ask the group what animals they can name, and then I work my way through a selection of animals and how they'd play football. For example, we start by being giraffes, play for a short period of time, then ask the group for another animal. Be mindful of the children's concentration spans and don't overload with many animals at once. Introduce them one by one and recap often what each animal needs to do, working your way up to a list of animals you can call for them to demonstrate behaviors for. Be sure to join in and have fun—the children will copy you!

BEHAVIORS

Giraffe: Hold the ball above your head and walk on your tiptoes, making yourself as tall as you can.

Elephants: Try to hold the ball in the palm of your hand while extending your arm out as if it's the elephant's trunk. Take big, heavy, and slow steps.

Lion: Hold the ball under one arm and run as fast as you can (carefully) while roaring like a lion. Who has the loudest roar?

VARIATIONS

- Include parents or guardians in the session, to demonstrate positive examples for the players.

- Challenge the players to show you what you could do for a certain animal. Slither like a snake, hold the ball like a tortoise's shell, and dribble the ball at your feet while you flap your wings like a bird! They'll come up with great and imaginative ways. Just be sure that they play and create ways to move safely.

- Pretend the goals circulated around the area are feeding stations for the animals and tell players to feed the animals by kicking the ball into the goal.

COMPONENT 2: FIND NEMO

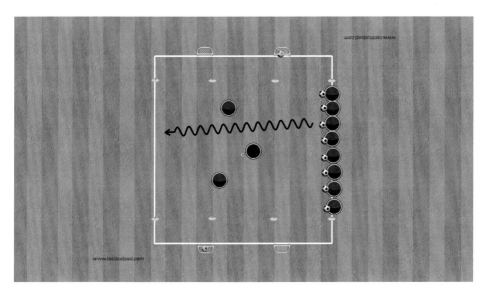

Figure 68. The players are each Nemo, trying to swim through the East Australian Current, past Bruce the Shark.

ENVIRONMENT

Component 1 very much works in isolation as a fun introductory activity. Now you start to build the story with a favorite animal character: Nemo. In this fun Find Nemo game, the children line up and need to race through the East Australian Current as quickly as possible by running from one side of the area to the other. With time and repetition, this exercise can ideally be done with a ball at their feet. The ball could be the swim mask from the movie, with the address of where they're going to on it—does anyone remember the address? Progress by having the coach becoming Bruce the Shark in the middle of the sea, trying to stop the players (Nemo or Dory—they can pick whomever they want to be) from getting across the area.

BEHAVIORS

These games are all about fun and developing a relationship with the ball. Try to do as many games with a ball each as possible and occasionally games with a ball between two, in an effort to encourage teamwork and sharing. With time, players should problem solve that smaller touches and close control of the ball will help them keep it away from the sharks and be able to change direction and manipulate the ball better.

VARIATIONS

- Include parents or guardians in the session, to demonstrate positive examples for the players.

- Allow some players to be Bruce the Shark.

- Progress to adding jellyfish. If Bruce gets a player's ball, that player joins Bruce in the middle of the area as a jellyfish. I implement this by asking players to sit on the ground and tackle with their arms or legs, but again, ensure that the group you're working with can carry this out safely.

- If possible, add goals at the end of the area that players can shoot into when they arrive at the other end—a fun incentive for the players and more opportunities to work on kicking the ball.

COMPONENT 3: FIND NEMO, VERSION TWO

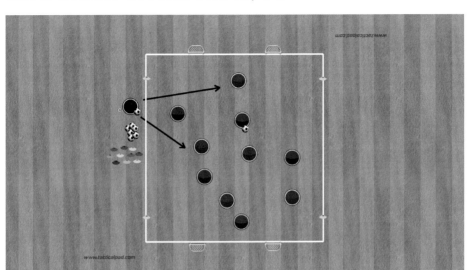

Figure 69. Players get sent off to the scoreboard as a reward and have a chance to flip over a cone to find Nemo (a coin or keyring).

ENVIRONMENT

This game is an introduction to playing the game of football. Of course, many players will find it too challenging or complicated, but drip feeding in content from the Scoreboard Soccer curriculum will help with the transition between the development phases of Love Football and Play Football.

Find Nemo is a fun scoreboard game. Create the Great Barrier Reef by using a variety of different-color cones and explain to the players that while they're playing the games, you'll hide Nemo under a cone (you may use a coin or what I use—a small keyring of Nemo). Use the scoreboard to reward goal scoring and praise effort, such as skill, attitude, and listening skills, by letting players come over and quickly flip a cone to see if they can find Nemo. The first team to find Nemo wins, so the more players score, work hard, and display a good attitude, the more the coach will send them to the scoreboard, and the greater chance they'll have to find Nemo and win the game for their team. Once a player finds Nemo, reset the scoreboard and play again.

BEHAVIORS

When a player finds Nemo, it's always a good idea to ask them this in front of the group: "Why did I send you to the scoreboard?" and when they respond along the lines of "I said 'Well done' to my teammate" or "because you said I was trying my hardest," the rest of the group will take note that these are the behaviors to work on during the game. Fun, as always, is the key behavior we seek during this game, and if it isn't fun or is proving too challenging with the group, never hesitate to fall back on some free play or move to a tried and tested game they enjoy. You can keep revisiting game-based activities over time. Patience is crucial when working with this age group.

VARIATIONS

- Include parents or guardians in the session, to demonstrate positive examples for the players.

- When first introducing game-based activities to this age group, I tend to make the games multigoal games—surrounding the pitch with four, six, or eight goals and letting players know that they can score in any goal. Kicking, running, and smiling are important with this age group; the concept of which way to shoot (easy enough to pick up later) isn't.

- Play with not only multigoals but also multiballs. This isn't an important soccer match the children are playing; it's a fun environment where you want all of them to chase and touch the ball—and hopefully score a goal. As shown in figure 69, I don't hesitate to pass in three or four balls at one time.

COMPONENT 4: DUCK, DUCK, GOOSE

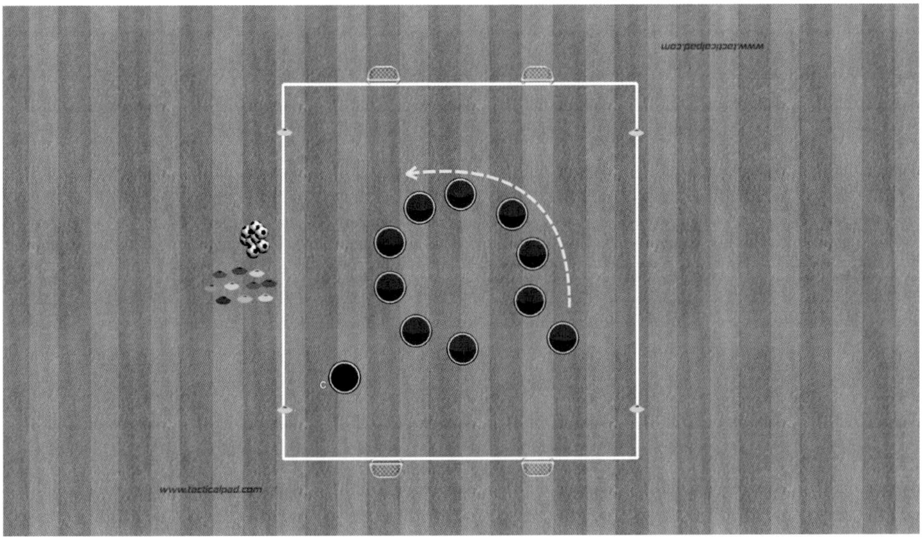

Figure 70. Operate a game of duck, duck, goose. You can incorporate soccer elements if you wish.

ENVIRONMENT

As coaches, we have a wonderful opportunity to educate children, not just about soccer but about a whole variety of things. I like to finish this session by recapping some of the animals we acted out, the noises they make, and what everyone's favorite animal is. I then lead this into a game of duck, duck, goose, a tried and tested game that children always enjoy and will send them off with smiles on their faces and looking forward to the next session. The players sit in a circle while a selected player walks around the group, tapping each person on the head and saying "duck." Whenever the player wants to, they tap someone and say "goose." The goose must chase the player who's trying to get all the way around the circle and back to the goose's spot without being captured. Make sure every player gets a turn as both the goose and the person being chased.

BEHAVIORS

Despite there being minimal physical exertion in this game, the game aids many aspects of social development—displaying confidence and decision-making as players circle the group to pick a goose and perhaps even thinking strategically about whom they should pick for the best chance to return to their spot without being captured. This is a fun game that will keep all children involved and make the group comfortable with one another.

VARIATIONS

- Include parents or guardians in the session, to demonstrate positive examples for the players.

- You can be creative and think of a football variation to this classic children's game. For example, when a child picks a goose, the first child runs around the circle and back to their place but must do so before the goose scores a goal. Situate balls in front of each goal for this adaptation.

CURRICULUM: Storybook Soccer

SESSION: 3

AGE: 4–12

STAGE: Love Football

THEMES: Fun, Balance, Cognitive Skills, Cars

COMPONENT 1: TAG

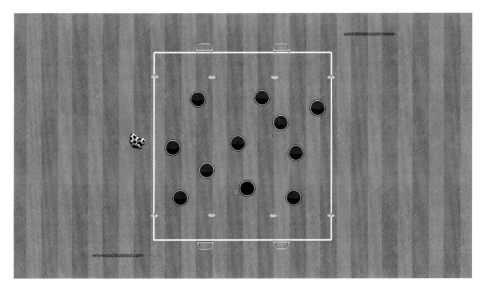

Figure 71. Tag games are great with younger players.

ENVIRONMENT

Younger children in particular tend to find games of tag good fun, and I use them often when coaching. There's a wide variety of tag games—they tend to use little to no equipment and are easy to understand and implement. If, at any point in a session, I need something to recapture the players' attention, I often have them play tag. In this particular session, after free play, I start with a game of tunnel tag—tagged players need to stand with their legs open and become free only after another player crawls between their legs. Change the tagger frequently, and after each round, you may add more taggers to make the game increasingly challenging.

BEHAVIORS

Tag games are great for developing skills such as agility, balance, and special awareness. I find that tag games can also give you a platform to speak about some basic but important topics for young children:

- Taking turns (to be the tagger)

- Being honest (if you're tagged)

- Being fair (not always chasing the same person)

VARIATIONS

- Include parents or guardians in the session, to demonstrate positive examples for the players.

- Depending on the age and stage of the group, play such that each player has a ball and that if the tagger kicks a player's ball, that's equivalent to getting tagged. For a player to become free, someone must pass a ball through that player's legs.

- There are a variety of tag games, such as freeze tag, toilet tag, and chain tag. The players may even be able to show you some tag games they know and enjoy.

COMPONENT 2: TRAFFIC LIGHT

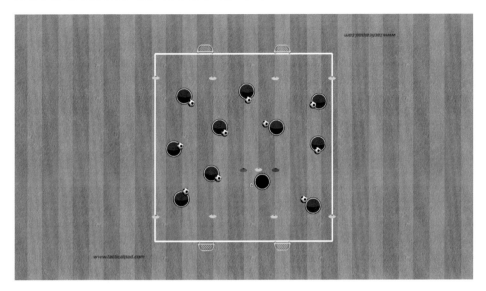

Figure 72. The coach calls out (or holds up the appropriate cone for) the colors of the traffic light (red, yellow, and green), with different meanings for each.

ENVIRONMENT

For this session, the story is based on cars. Similar sessions can be done around other methods of transportation, such as trains, planes, or boats. The players get in their race car (dribble the ball) and move around the racetrack, making sure they don't crash their car. Beeping their horn (making a beeping noise) helps let other drivers know that they're nearby! One by one, the coach introduces traffic lights to work on different skills.

- Red: stop

- Yellow: slow down

- Green: go

I've found it helpful to introduce the traffic-light colors one at a time to allow players to work on these skills in isolation before progressing to interchanging the light you're calling out. If nothing else, introducing the lights one by one helps prolong the activity and avoids too much instruction at once.

BEHAVIORS

When the coach shouts "red light," the players try to stop the ball. Congratulate those who try their best to put their foot on the ball and stop it from rolling. Encourage and help those who need it. When calling "yellow light," players adjust their speed to take small and slow touches. As the coach, give a visual demonstration of this technique as you call the command. Be sure to congratulate those trying their best and to be patient with those who perhaps use their hands from time to time. For "green light," players move a bit faster, and with time, coach them to find the balance of driving fast but with the ball under control to avoid crashing.

VARIATIONS

- Include parents or guardians in the session, to demonstrate positive examples for the players.

- After some practice, the group may be able to do a variation that involves mixing the commands up. For example, green could mean stop, and red could mean go.

- A progression to this exercise would be to have the coach simply hold up the cone instead of calling out the traffic-light color, challenging players to dribble while scanning and looking around the area.

- You can introduce things like speed bumps, cones that players need to jump over by holding the ball between both legs and jumping, or traffic circles, larger cones players need to dribble around.

COMPONENT 3: POLICE CAR

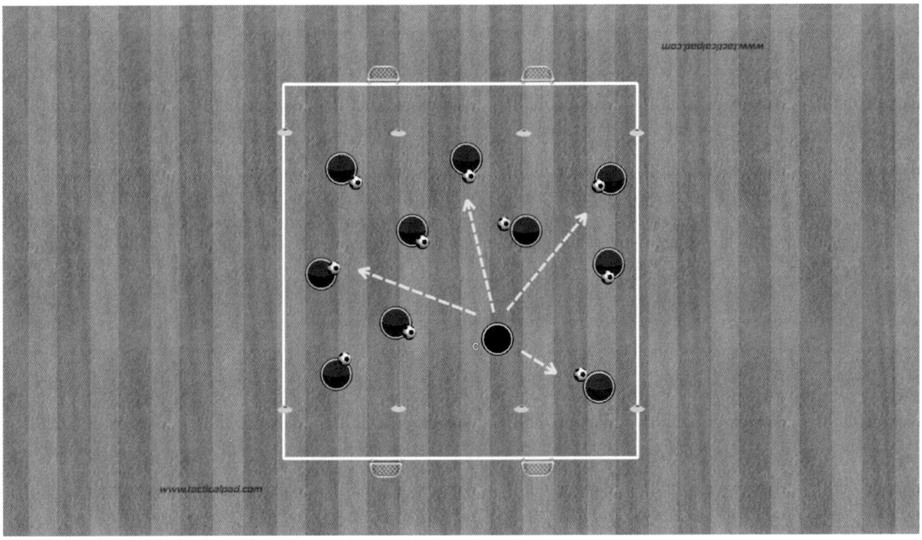

Figure 73. Players' cars now interact with a police car that tries to write a ticket (by kicking the player's ball). You can add many other fun elements to this game.

ENVIRONMENT

This game is called "Police Car." The coach now chases players' cars to try to give them a ticket by kicking their ball. The challenge for players is to drive (dribble) around the area and try not to get caught by the police car and not crash into another car. You may continue the traffic-light theme also, making them look out for red lights. I find that keeping the red light active throughout the session helps bring the players' attention back to the coach when necessary.

BEHAVIORS

This game gives players more of an opportunity to get familiar with the ball, be aware of their surroundings, and have fun. Increase the levels of fun in this activity by asking players to make the noise their race cars would make when speeding around the area (*zoom, zoom*!) and beeping their horns (*honk, honk*!). If players want to take turns being the police cars, they can also make the sound of the siren (*wee-oo, wee-oo*!).

VARIATIONS

- Include parents or guardians in the session, to demonstrate positive examples for the players.

- A fun variation is to have players go from trying not to crash their car to playing a game of bumper cars. Give the players thirty seconds to crash into as many cars as they can. This is a fun environment, and the players won't realize the skill involved in turning to find another car, communicating with other drivers, dribbling toward one another, and passing the balls into one another—not forgetting to shout "*crash*!"

- Every time I deliver this component, I find new fun things to add to the environment. The goals become gas stations for players to kick the ball into and refuel the car. I put ladders on the pitch to replicate a crosswalk that players can try to go through, or I use cones to create a pretend car wash or drive-through restaurant. Be creative and their imaginations will do the rest.

COMPONENT 4: WHAT'S THE TIME, MRS. [OR MR.] WOLF?

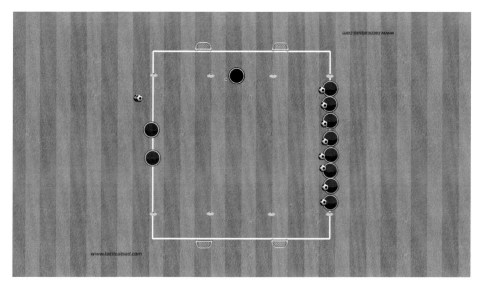

Figure 74. Players play a version of "What's the time, Mrs. [or Mr.] Wolf?" moving across the field with a number of touches that matches the time the wolf (or wolves) has declared it.

ENVIRONMENT

Similar to how storybook session 2 ends with duck, duck, goose, I finish this session with a tried and tested game that the players I work with always request. This game ensures that they leave with a smile on their faces and look forward to the next session. This is a game of "What's the time, Mrs. [or Mr.] Wolf?" Sometimes we play it without the ball, but more often than not, I like to keep the ball involved. I also like to have two wolves so the children can work together. The players with the ball shout to ask the time (normally I need to give them a three-two-one countdown), and the wolves reply with a time, such as two o'clock or five o'clock. This is how many touches the players take before stopping the ball. I tend to join the group and challenge them to keep in line with me. At the shout of "Dinner time!" the wolves try to get someone's ball before the players can get back to the den, which is the line they started at.

BEHAVIORS

Small and controlled touches, stopping the ball, and being ready to turn with the ball are all crucial skills hidden within this fun game. On the call of "Dinner time," it becomes more about moving a bit faster with the ball and keeping it away from the wolf (defender). With time, try to promote behaviors, such as collaboration. Can the players all shout together to ask the time? Can the wolves agree on a time to call? As time passes and they become familiar with the game, can the players start to take ownership of setting up and playing the game? As the coach, you're always on hand to help, but start to drip feed the idea of player autonomy through activities like this.

VARIATIONS

- Include parents or guardians in the session, to demonstrate positive examples for the players.

- The defenders (wolves) may play this game with or without the ball.

- You may twist the terminology in the game to suit your storybook theme, such as "What's the time, Mrs. Dinosaur?" or "What's the time, Mr. Alien?"

CURRICULUM: Storybook Soccer

SESSION: 4

AGE: 4–12

STAGE: Love Football

THEMES: Fun, Passing, Confidence, Spaceships

COMPONENT 1: HITTING THE CONES

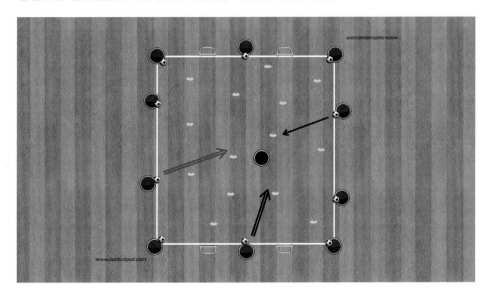

Figure 75. Players kick their ball to try to hit a cone for a point.

ENVIRONMENT

As mentioned, I start most sessions with players of this age or stage with unstructured free play. In this session, we then move into this fun activity, which can be, for some players, an introduction to passing the ball. Outside the playing area (make the size appropriate for the age and stage of the players), everyone has a ball, and the aim is to pass the ball to hit a cone, which results in a point. The players run in to collect their ball and bring it back for another shot. To ensure the safety of all players, be sure to stipulate that the ball must stay on the ground.

BEHAVIORS

This is a good environment to introduce the concept of aiming when kicking the ball. Players may be too busy having fun and celebrating when they hit a cone to realize that they're taking their time to look where the cone is, line up their shot, then strike the ball in that direction. The concept of using the inside of the foot and aiming with the standing foot, among other concepts, may come with time but, initially, just embrace them being mindful of aiming and kicking the ball.

VARIATIONS

- Include parents or guardians in the session, to demonstrate positive examples for the players.

- This is an easy environment to incorporate a race. Challenge players to get as many points as they can in thirty seconds. Play again, and have them try to beat their score.

- As opposed to hitting a cone, one week you might play such that it's a point if their ball finishes still touching a cone. This would be a more advanced variation in regard to using the right amount of power when kicking the ball.

- Use small traffic cones that players can knock over or place balls to hit off the cones, which they may find more fun.

- One week, you may play a game of "How many cones can you hit in a row?" This would involve passing from the outside of the area, hitting a cone (one point), and taking a second shot from where the first shot lands. If a player hits a cone again, that's two points, and if they hit it again, it's three. Once a player misses, they go back outside the area and see if they can hit more in a row the next time.

COMPONENT 2: VOLCANOES AND SPACESHIPS

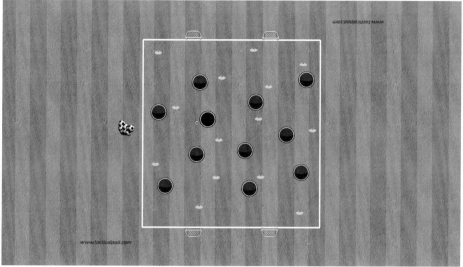

Figure 76. Players race to flip cones from spaceships to volcanoes or volcanoes to spaceships.

ENVIRONMENT

The story starts here with Spaceships vs. Volcanoes. The cones all around the area (already set up from component 1) are either sitting right side up (volcanoes) or upside down (spaceships). Players run around the area and flip over as many cones as they can—either turning volcanoes into spaceships or vice versa. Keep players engaged by challenging them to do as many as they can in twenty seconds. Ask them their scores, play again, and see if they can beat their previous scores. As a coach, you should play, too, so they can see you work hard and have fun while playing.

BEHAVIORS

Players will be working on change of direction, acceleration, and motor skills, such as bending, turning, starting, and stopping. If you challenge players to keep their score, they'll also be working on counting. They'll also be crucially scanning the area and being careful not to bang into anyone. It's important as coaches to make sure the players are always safe within the environment.

VARIATIONS

- Include parents or guardians in the session, to demonstrate positive examples for the players.

- You may progress to playing this game with a ball. Players dribble to a cone, stop the ball, flip the cones, then move to the next one to get another point.

- One week, you might put the players into two teams—with one team being the volcanoes trying to get all cones right side up and the other team (the spaceships) trying to turn them over.

- You may work the players as one big team. Start all cones as spaceships, and time the players to see how quickly they can turn them all into volcanoes. Time them again to flip them back and see if they can work together to beat their previous time. Again, this can also be done with the ball, and it's great for encouraging effort and teamwork.

COMPONENT 3: LAVA

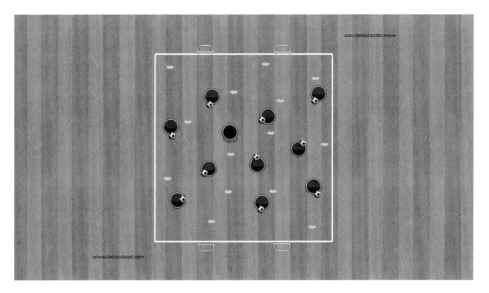

Figure 77. Players work to avoid lava (bibs) being thrown at their balls by the coach.

ENVIRONMENT

Now ask the players, "What do we find in volcanoes?" Lava! In this game, the players fly their spaceships (dribble the ball) and need to watch out for the lava (bibs) coming out of all the volcanoes on the pitch. The coach runs around with bibs in their hands and tries to throw the bibs and hit the player's ball (lava to hit the spaceship). If a spaceship is struck by lava, the player must do three star jumps before being able to fly (dribble) again. Depending on the age and stage of the players, you may want to play this game as a continuation of the previous component, so players are still trying to flip cones and get points.

BEHAVIORS

Players will be flying their spaceships around the area and trying to avoid the lava, but as coaches, we know that they're dribbling their ball with close control and protecting it by moving away from danger. This environment allows coaches to challenge players who are showing a more advanced level of dribbling—throwing bibs at the ball with more intent, so players need to twist and turn away. It also allows coaches to embed some basic coaching for those who perhaps take touches of the ball that are too heavy, and you can guide them toward smaller, more-controlled touches so it's harder for you to hit their ball with the bib.

VARIATIONS

- Include parents or guardians in the session, to demonstrate positive examples for the players.

- Ask the players if anyone wants to be the lava thrower and let them have turns being catchers.

- Instead of star jumps, players can take five quick touches of the ball (toe taps, for example).

- This game can be progressed to become like tunnel tag (as described in Storybook Soccer session 3, component 1). If a player is hit by lava, they hold the ball above their head and open their legs. A teammate can free them by passing the ball under their legs.

COMPONENT 4: VOLCANOES VS. SPACESHIPS

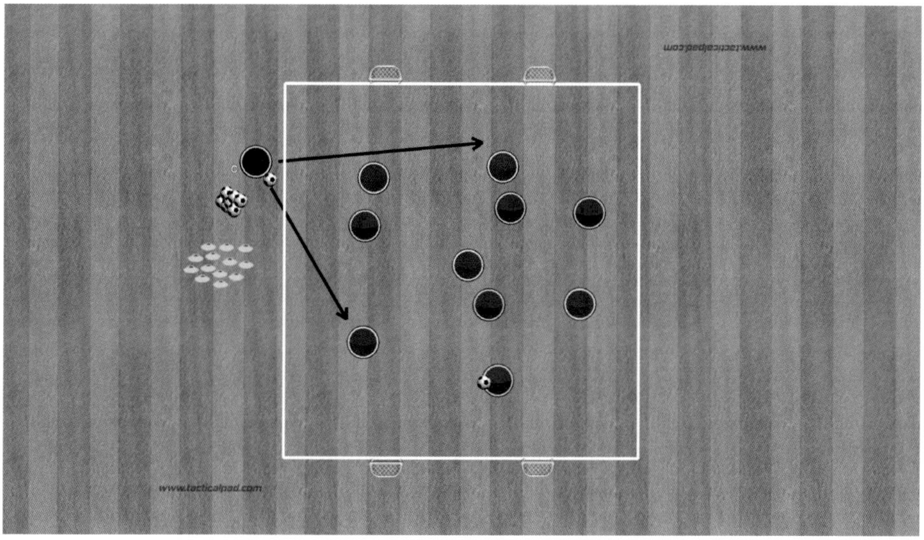

Figure 78. This Scoreboard Soccer game works well with young players.

ENVIRONMENT

Split the group into two teams—the volcanoes and the spaceships. Half the cones at the side of the pitch start upside down (spaceships) while the other half start right side up (volcanoes). Play small-sided games for a set amount of time, with the aim being for the teams to get as many cones representing their team as possible. If they score and are on the volcanoes team, for example, they quickly run to the scoreboard to turn a cone that's upside down to right side up, then quickly return to the pitch. The team with the most— spaceships or volcanoes—after the set time limit wins the game, and you can reset the scoreboard and play again.

BEHAVIORS

This game is an introduction to playing soccer. As described throughout the book, I look at the stage of players in three key phases: love soccer, play soccer, learn soccer. These phases need to overlap frequently to help the transition from one phase to the other. Drip feed some ideas from the Scoreboard Soccer curriculum into the Storybook Soccer curriculum and vice versa. When playing these games with younger players, I tend to amplify the number of opportunities to score by not making the games directional. You can score in any goal around the pitch. I also tend to utilize a multiball system, passing balls into the game to give more players touches of the ball. And crucially, I praise the process as opposed to the outcome. If a player tried their best or shows improvement from the previous week in regard to engagement with the ball, I praise them by asking them to come to the scoreboard and flip a cone for their team.

VARIATIONS

- Include parents or guardians in the session, to demonstrate positive examples for the players.

- With time and more exposure to small-sided or scoreboard games where you can start to make it more directional. Another benefit of scoreboard games is that you can easily praise a young player for shooting the correct way, by saying "Well done" and sending them to the scoreboard.

- The Volcanoes vs. Spaceships scoreboard game is used in this session to link in with the story this week. Keep in mind that there are many creative scoreboard games that the younger players really enjoy, especially Connect Four, Find Nemo, and Splat Attack.

CURRICULUM: Storybook Soccer

SESSION: 5

AGE: 4–12

STAGE: Love Football

THEMES: Fun, Imagination, Conentration, Toys

COMPONENT 1: TAIL TAG

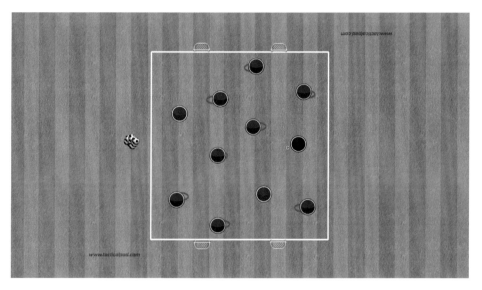

Figure 79. Taggers for tail tag try to catch the "tails" (bibs hanging out of the back of players' shorts).

ENVIRONMENT

In tail tag, the players run freely with a bib hanging out the back of their shorts, representing a tail. Choose an appropriate number of taggers who need to try and catch the tails. When a player loses their tail, they join the catchers. Play until all tails have been caught, then choose new catchers and start again.

BEHAVIORS

Like all tag games, young players tend to understand the concepts quickly and can therefore spend more time running and being physically active. Once players have played this game a few times, you may introduce the ball. The introduction of the ball progresses this activity to encourage constant twisting, turning, and foot skills as players need to protect both their tail (from the catcher) and the ball (from the coach). This is how I play this game when using the ball, and it's worked well.

VARIATIONS

- Include parents or guardians in the session, to demonstrate positive examples for the players.

- When a catcher gets a player's tail, the catcher gives it back, but the player needs to do three star jumps before joining the game again. Catchers can keep track of how many they catch in a certain time limit.

- Play tail tag with all players dribbling a ball. It may take a lot of time and patience for the younger players to be able to dribble and protect their tails at the same time.

COMPONENT 2: TOY STORY

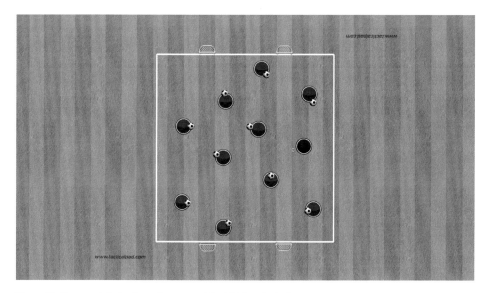

Figure 80. Players mimic Toy Story characters while dribbling the ball.

ENVIRONMENT

Each player has a ball, and you introduce different characters for the players to try and imitate.

- Woody or Jessie: Players shout "Yeehaw!" and dribble while pretending to swing a lasso above their heads.

- Buzz: Players shout "To infinity and beyond!" and dribble with their arms out wide like they're flying.

- Slinky Dog: Two players dribble a ball while holding hands as if they're the head and the tail of the dachshund.

You (or the players) may be able to think of other creative ways to be other Toy Story characters, such as Rex, Little Bo-Peep, and Forky.

BEHAVIORS

Different characters bring different behaviors for the players to work on. Try to incorporate as many touches of the ball as possible, and the characters should allow you to facilitate some hidden learning in regard to players using their balance, coordination, and imagination.

VARIATIONS

- Include parents or guardians in the session, to demonstrate positive examples for the players.

COMPONENT 3: "ANDY'S COMING!"

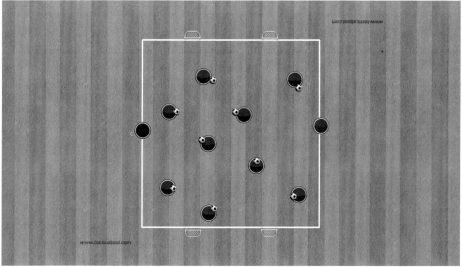

Figure 81. Players continue acting like Toy Story characters but await the coach announcing "Andy's coming!" where they have to stop the ball, lie down, and freeze.

ENVIRONMENT

This game is a continuation of component 2. Now that the players have worked on different ways of imitating the toys, they pick their favorite toy and move in that fashion, dribbling, playing, and having as much fun as they can while Andy (the coach) is "out of the room." When the coach shouts, "Andy's coming!" that means the coach is entering the "room," so the toys need to immediately stop what they're doing. Encourage the players to stop the ball, carefully lie on the ground, and make sure Andy doesn't catch any of the toys moving! If everyone is still, Andy will leave the room, and they can play again. If you catch a player moving or being the last one to stop, they'll be Andy for the next round. The children really enjoy taking a turn as Andy, covering their eyes and shouting "Andy's coming!"

BEHAVIORS

It's important that players form a relationship with the ball at this age and stage. This is another activity where the ball represents fun, and they'll get a lot of touches while keeping it under control, ready to stop the ball whenever Andy enters the room. Awareness is a big part of this exercise as players dribble around, keeping an eye on when Andy might enter the room.

VARIATIONS

- Include parents or guardians in the session, to demonstrate positive examples for the players.

- The young players I've done this game with have loved it when I've used music to represent Andy. If you're able to play "You've Got a Friend in Me," when you pause the music, they must freeze. Players really enjoy this aspect.

COMPONENT 4: TIDY THE TOYS

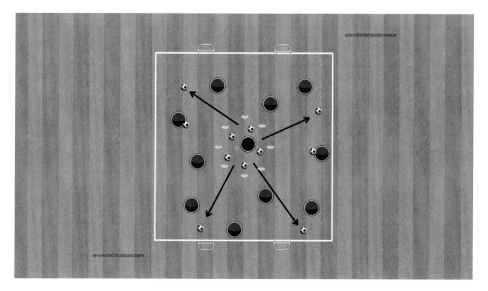

Figure 82. Players work to collect balls and bring them to the center.

ENVIRONMENT

This activity starts with the players standing in the toy box (coned area), shown in figure 82, with toys (balls) spread around the surrounding area. Players must collect toys and dribble them back to the central area, stopping the toy in the area and going to collect another toy. Within a set time limit, the players must get as many toys back into the central toy box as possible. The coach in the area will be Sid, the boy next door in the *Toy Story* film, who throws all the toys out of the toy box, making it harder for the players. After the time limit, count up to see who won. Did the players get more toys in the toy box, or did Sid manage to kick the majority out?

BEHAVIORS

Behaviors being worked on here include running, turning, dribbling, and even passing—if you allow players to pass the balls back into the central area. Teamwork is also important as the players collaborate to get all the balls into the central area.

VARIATIONS

- Include parents or guardians in the session, to demonstrate positive examples for the players.

- You may allow players to throw, bounce, or roll the balls back to work on different motor skills.

- Instead of using a central area, you could use the goals around the outside of the pitch, with Sid running around and emptying the balls out of the goals.

- Pick two or three players to be Sid in the middle, working on kicking the balls as far away as they can.

THE CURRICULUM

SCOREBOARD SOCCER

Creating fun and conducive learning environments to promote learning through trial and error. Show patience and support while giving players space to problem solve. For all components and sessions, if you don't have goals or cones, bibs for goalposts are fine.

SCOREBOARD SOCCER—INTRODUCTORY PRACTICE

I often task players with organizing player-led games as an introductory activity. Essentially, when they arrive at training, they set up games among themselves and play, taking complete ownership of the environment.

In regard to the Scoreboard Soccer curriculum that follows, I recommend building in frequent player-led games. Let the players play and be themselves. As a coach, be on hand to ensure that they're all safe and having fun within the environment. I tend to start most sessions in this curriculum with games. At times, I incorporate games during or at the end of the session also. I think it's a good coaching tool for if you feel that the players are becoming disengaged or that your session component isn't working the way you'd like—break into games for a short time before moving onto the next component.

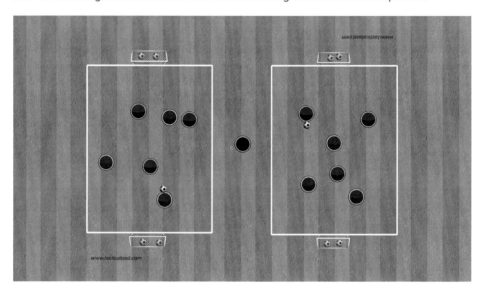

Figure 83. Scoreboard soccer warm-up.

CURRICULUM: Scoreboard Soccer

SESSION: 1

AGE: 8–16

STAGE: Play Football

THEMES: Passing, Possession, Awareness, Defending, Pressing

COMPONENT 1: WORK TOGETHER

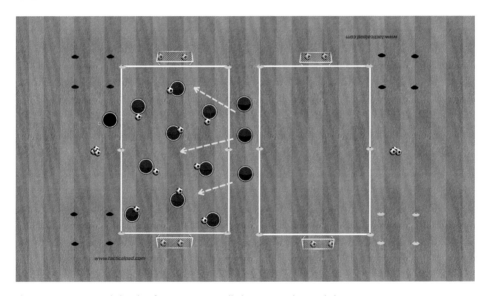

Figure 84. Set up two pitches, but for component 1, all players use only one pitch.

ENVIRONMENT

Set up two pitches as shown in figure 84, with all players using one pitch for component 1. Start by having all players dribbling in this area and encourage close control and different skill moves. Progress to having three defenders come off the pitch. On the coach's command, the defenders enter the pitch and try to kick all balls off the pitch. Each player's aim is to keep their ball away from the defenders, using their close control and skill moves. When a player has their ball stolen and kicked off the pitch, the player remains on the pitch and helps their teammates to keep balls on the pitch; therefore, the drill becomes more about passing and moving as well as scanning, communicating, and spreading out, to keep as many balls on the pitch and away from the defenders as

possible. Add competition by saying the defenders have two minutes to knock all balls off the pitch. The attackers win the game by having at least one ball on the pitch at the end of the set time limit. Playing for a record number of balls the players can still have on the pitch after two minutes is a great challenge to set for the players.

BEHAVIORS

Initially, players must work on close control, changing direction and acceleration to move away from the defenders, who in turn will be working on their 1v1 defending to win the ball. As balls start to be eliminated from the game, scanning and communication become crucial for the team in possession—seeking to help teammates or calling for help. Bunching together is likely to make it easy for the defenders; however, always moving into space and looking to receive the ball in areas farther from the defenders will make it difficult for the defenders to win the ball. The behaviors you would encourage from the defenders include working together, hunting in packs, and communicating to set traps to win the ball. If a teammate is pressing, can the defender offering cover tell that teammate what way to show the next pass and, therefore, be in the best position to press the next pass and maybe win the ball?

VARIATIONS

- Figure 84 shows component 1 with twelve players but can be easily adapted. If you have a large number, split the group in two and have the game running on both pitches.

- Change the defenders after each round.

- Increase or decrease the number of defenders in the game.

- Challenge the defenders further by asking them to win the ball and pass it into the goals surrounding the pitch.

- Increase or decrease the area size depending on the age and stage of the players you're working with.

- Modify the time limit for each game.

COMPONENT 2: PASSING SCOREBOARD

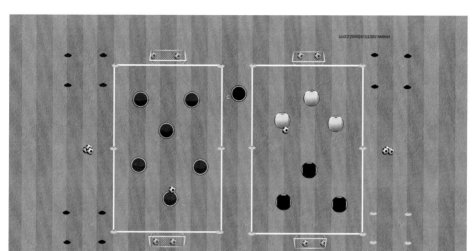

Figure 85. Praised players get one shot to pass into their team's scoreboard from an invisible alignment with the yellow cone.

ENVIRONMENT

Split the group into teams and play small-sided games on each pitch. You might place bibs in each goal before the start of the session, to minimize time getting set up and allow for a quick start of the games. Progress each game by introducing passing scoreboards. When a coach rewards a player for positive play or conduct, the player attempts to pass a ball into their scoreboard (from in line with the yellow cone, as shown in fig. 85). The team with the most balls in their scoreboard after the allocated game time wins. If all balls are gone from the middle area, allow teams to attempt to pass from the opposition's scoreboard into theirs. When the time is up, rotate the teams to allow for different opposition. Have the players reset the scoreboards before starting a new game.

BEHAVIORS

As the scoreboard's focus is passing, you could praise passing in the game. Scanning, communicating, and moving into space should be behaviors consistently praised from component 1, and you may reward this behavior in the game by congratulating players and sending them to the scoreboard. Good 1v1 defending or team pressing might also be something you praise. This is also a key behavior from component 1. The use of the scoreboard allows for many overloads and underloads on the pitch, aiming to allow players to work on not only their passing and weight of pass but their decision-making also.

VARIATIONS

- Figure 85 shows 3v3, but depending on your numbers, this could be 4v4, 5v5, or if you have an odd number, a playmaker situation.

- Encourage players to take a slight touch of the ball before they attempt to pass into their scoreboard, to ensure that they're working on passing a moving ball.

- If two teams finish in a tie for the most balls in their scoreboard, you can use the scoreboard as a fun tiebreaker game, lining the players up to take a pass each, where the first to miss loses, like a penalty shootout but using the passing scoreboard.

- Enhance the competition aspect by having a tournament, with every team playing each other once and keeping score. Remember, these games are about praising positive behaviors—things like teamwork and sportsmanship can lead to winning scoreboard games.

COMPONENT 3: KEEP THE BALL

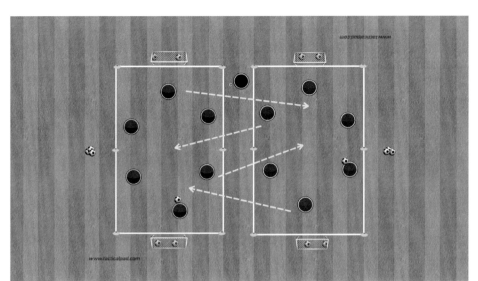

Figure 86. On the coach's command, two defenders from each team press the other team in an attempt to win the ball.

ENVIRONMENT

Split the group into two teams, one on each pitch, with both teams passing and moving with a ball on their pitch. On the coach's command, two defenders from each team press the other team in an attempt to win the ball. The first team to win the ball wins a point. You may choose to number the players and shout what numbers are to press. At the coach's discretion, the coach might shout one or two numbers or even more if there are more players and you want to challenge the passing of the team with the ball. While a coach facilitates this practice, another coach can be picking up the cones from the previous game, to ensure a smooth transition between session components.

BEHAVIORS

As is consistent with the rest of this session, this component calls for players to focus on passing the ball firmly, moving to create passing lanes, and constantly scanning to assess passing options and where the defenders are, to avoid the danger of losing the ball. I've delivered this where another coach and I decided prior to the session that I'd focus on the passing and possession of the team with the ball while they focused on the 1v1 defending and pressing of the players without the ball, both aspects of the game complementing and challenging each other.

VARIATIONS

- Increase the tempo of passing by adding a second way to win the game: after ten passes, the players can finish in either goal—the first team to do so wins.

- A good adaptation to this exercise is to deliver it similar to component 1. All players could have a ball, and the defenders could go over and try to knock all balls out while the attacking teams' players try to keep as many in the area as possible. The first set of defenders to knock out all the balls or the attacking team with the most balls left after a set time limit is the winner.

- Challenge players to pass and move. One way to do this with younger players is to ask them to follow their pass.

COMPONENT 4: PLAY A GAME

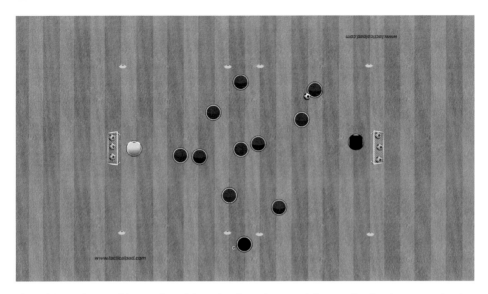

Figure 87. Introduce conditions, such as giving points for each pass and then transforming those pass points into goals once the team scores a goal.

ENVIRONMENT

By simply picking up a couple of cones and moving the goals, you can now create a game. You may be able to set this up while the players are taking part in the previous component. Try to minimize setup time and maximize activity throughout all sessions. You may decide to simply let the session finish with a normal game of football and just rotate the goalkeepers frequently, but you can introduce a condition that brings the theme of the session to the surface. An example condition here would be that every pass is a point, and if a player scores, those points turn into goals. For example, a move that involves five passes and a goal would be worth five goals; a move that involves ten passes and a goal is worth ten points.

BEHAVIORS

The condition described in this component will bring passing, moving, scanning, and importantly, decision-making to the surface. Players won't want to give up the ball easily if they've amassed fifteen points through a long passing sequence; they'll be keen to finish this sequence with a goal. This will also help decision-making when it comes to finishing—for example, not trying to hit the ball too hard when a passed shot would bring more success.

VARIATIONS

- Players who play as goalkeepers may want to stay in goal for the majority of the game.

- In a 6v6 game, use the passing scoreboard idea from component 2.

- Play without any conditions.

CURRICULUM: Scoreboard Soccer

SESSION: 2

AGE: 8–16

STAGE: Play Football

THEMES: Dribbling, 1v1, 2v2, Overloads, Underloads

COMPONENT 1: THROUGH THE MIDDLE

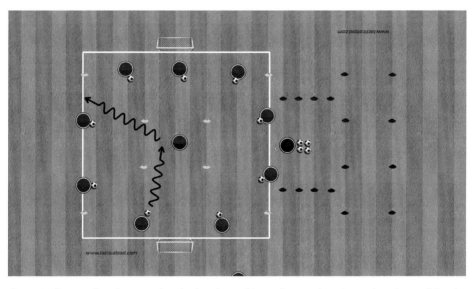

Figure 88. Players work on close control moving into the small box at the same time, then work on change of direction moving outside the small box.

ENVIRONMENT

Set up a small, five-by-five-yard box, surrounded by a larger, twenty-by-twenty-yard box. I set this up within the area of the pitch to save having to set the pitch up later and to ensure a quick transition between components. Have all players spread out around the larger box, with a ball each. This practice involves working on close control as all players enter the small box at the same time. Change of direction is then important to avoid players colliding with other players and to assist in them finding a way out of the small box before accelerating back to the outside of the larger box. Players work on a turn before repeating this sequence, constantly working on close control, change of direction, and change of speed to get through the small box as efficiently as possible.

BEHAVIORS

This environment allows the players to get a lot of touches of the ball. Encourage players to take small, slower touches as they approach the small box, lifting their heads after every couple of touches, to be aware of the traffic around them as they enter the box. Lifting their heads and scanning allows players to identify space to escape into when leaving the small box. They should do this with exaggerated skill moves and a slightly bigger touch to accelerate into space and race back to the edge of the larger square. Behaviors players can work on in this environment include close control, a variety of skill moves to change direction, and different turns when reaching the outside of the larger box.

VARIATIONS

- Alter the distances between cones to either make the area tighter, to stress close control, or to give players more ground to cover and drive into with the ball.

- As figure 88 shows, you can add a defender into the small, central box to give players less space to work within and stress scanning more to encourage awareness of where space and the defender are.

- Make the practice competitive to emphasize moving with the ball at pace. Challenge players to get through the small box as many times as possible within thirty seconds. Have them rest for ten seconds and play again, trying to beat their score.

COMPONENT 2: NUMBERS

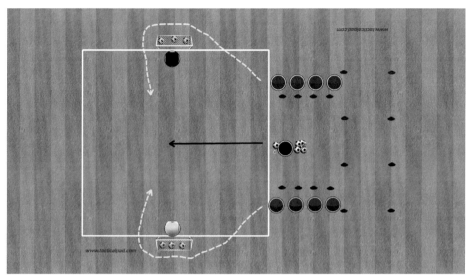

Figure 89. Players line up in single-file lines by team. When the coach passes a ball in, they shout a number, and that many players from each team run around their goal and onto the pitch for a game.

ENVIRONMENT

Players line up in single-file lines by team at the side of the pitch, with a goalkeeper in each goal. You can have regular goalkeepers, or players can take turns in goals. The coach has a supply of balls and passes one in and shouts a number. The number shouted signifies how many players from each team run around their goal and come on the pitch to play. This can create environments for players to work on various situations, such as 1v1, 2v2, 3v3, and 4v4. When the game is over, the players join their line again.

BEHAVIORS

When attacking in 1v1 situations, can players demonstrate the behaviors worked on in component 1—close control, change of direction, and change of pace? When defending in 1v1 situations, can players deny the opponent time and space and get their body between the ball and the goal, showing patience to frustrate the attacker and perhaps force an error or create an opportunity to win the ball? This environment gives players a lot of opportunities to problem solve different situations, and you might help by facilitating some guided discovery of the coaching points discussed in "The Coaching" section of this book.

VARIATIONS

- If a phase is over too quickly, the coach can pass in a "bonus ball," a second or third ball, to prolong the practice. It can also give you an opportunity to pass to a player whom you may want to get more touches of the ball.

- Keep score and implement the rule that when a team is three goals ahead the other team adds one player to every number shouted, creating overload and underload situations for players to work on.

COMPONENT 3: DRIBBLING SCOREBOARD

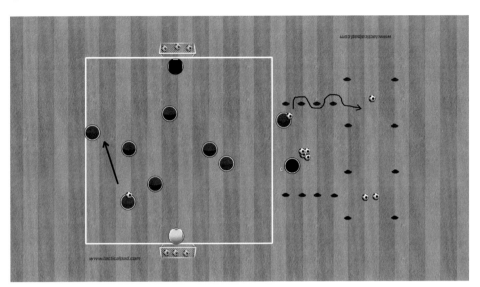

Figure 90. A rewarded player attempts a scoreboard point by dribbling around the cones. If they hit a cone, they return to the pitch without adding a point to their team's score.

ENVIRONMENT

The scoreboard in this game consists of two three-by-three-yard boxes. One box represents the red team's scoreboard, and the other represents the blue team's scoreboard. After scoring a goal in the game, the goal scorer rushes over and has one attempt to dribble a ball through a line of cones and into their team's scoreboard. If the player hits a cone before reaching the scoreboard, they must return the ball to the central pile and rejoin the game without getting that point. Players need to find the balance of dribbling fast to get a point and quickly get back on the pitch to help their team and also not rushing, losing control of the ball. When all the balls are in one of the scoreboards, the game ends, and teams count to see who wins. Reset the scoreboard to play again. At that point, you may want to mix up the teams or alternate opposition for the players if you have more than one pitch running at the same time.

BEHAVIORS

You may use the scoreboard to boost the confidence of certain players. If a player is struggling to get involved in the game, I find that telling them "Well done" and sending them to the scoreboard for simply getting on the ball can motivate them to get on the ball more often. Praise the process, not the outcome—for example, attempting to make forward passes or to get back and help their—successful or not—are behaviors worthy of praise.

VARIATIONS

- When a player comes to the scoreboard, you may challenge them to dribble with their nondominant foot for two additional points as opposed to just one, which is what they would get for using the foot they feel is their strongest.

- If you're working with an odd number of players, utilize a playmaker in the game or simply play with uneven teams.

COMPONENT 4: SCORE AND SWITCH

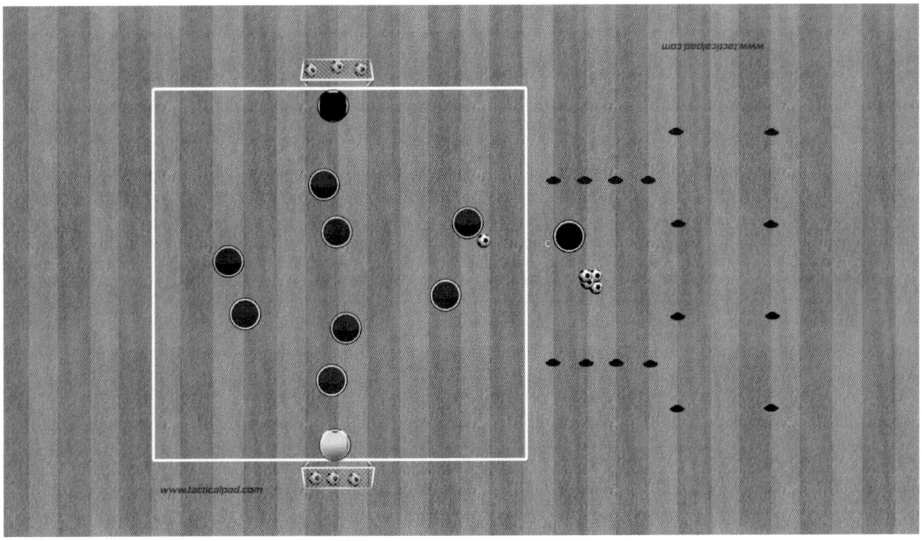

Figure 91. As soon as a team scores, the scoring team works to attack against the other goal, as the teams switch sides with each goal.

ENVIRONMENT

Finish with a game of football—you may choose to play without conditions and instruction. Alternatively, my players enjoy the condition that teams swap sides when a goal is scored. So, when a team scores, the players quickly grab the ball they scored with and immediately attack the other way. This is a fun way to build an environment that encourages quick solutions to goal, especially if you're playing with goalkeepers, as the goals will momentarily be empty while they swap sides.

BEHAVIORS

The score and keep-the-ball environment encourage behaviors such as positive attacking play and decision-making. Players may be more motivated and try their best to achieve things like keeping possession, passing to teammates who are in better positions to score, and finishing with composure and assurance so they can grab the ball and quickly start the next attack in the opposite direction.

VARIATIONS

- If you have players who play as goalkeepers, they may want to stay in goal for most of the game.

- In the 5v5 game, instead of the condition described above, ask the players if they want to continue the dribbling scoreboard idea from component 2.

- Play without conditions.

CURRICULUM: Scoreboard Soccer

SESSION: 3

AGE: 8–16

STAGE: Play Football

THEMES: Shooting, Passing, Defending, Goalkeepers, 1v1

COMPONENT 1: SHOOTING PRACTICE

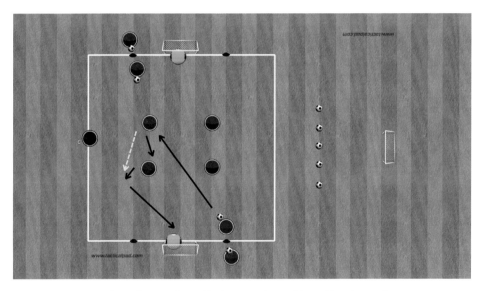

Figure 92. Both teams play at the same time, with players rotating positions with each new play.

ENVIRONMENT

This passing and shooting exercise allows for plenty of repetition for the attackers and goalkeepers. Both groups go at the same time, playing the first pass to the player farthest away, who then plays a wall pass with the player in front of them before shooting on goal. The rotation is as follows:

- The Initial passers become the layoff players.

- The layoff players move to become the shooters.

- The players who shot the ball collect their ball and join the line.

Be sure to have a suitable break between repetitions to make sure the environment is safe for players, as there's a lot of shooting in this practice. If you don't have a goalkeeper, the goalkeeper position can become part of the rotation, with players going into goal after they shoot and the goalkeepers getting the ball and joining the line.

BEHAVIORS

This environment forces the initial pass to be driven and accurate, into the feet of players' teammates. If that doesn't happen, the play may interfere with the other group's players, who are also working through the practice. Upon receiving the ball, the shooter will need the layoff player to move their feet to give a good angle for the layoff. The layoff should be in front of the shooter so they can step onto the ball and perhaps hit it the first time. Good practice when a player strikes the ball involves scanning to see where the goalkeeper is before getting the attacking player's head over the ball and striking through the ball cleanly, with the foot meeting as much of the surface area of the ball as possible. Striking just below the center of the ball and following through will help lift the ball off the ground, but players should avoid leaning back, lifting their head before connecting with the ball, or trying to hit it too hard. Striking the ball with clean contact and good technique is the important thing, and power will come with practice.

VARIATIONS

- In this practice, there's potential to vary the combination. Be experimental without overcomplicating things—you may find combinations that work well.

- Once players have a feel for the practice, you can facilitate a shooting competition between the two groups—for example, the first team to ten goals. Be sure to have goalkeepers or a player from each team go play against the opposition.

- Have an individual competition to see who scores the most goals in five minutes. You may add conditions, such as two points for hitting the goalpost but still going in, to encourage players to aim for the corners.

COMPONENT 2: SHOOTING SCOREBOARD

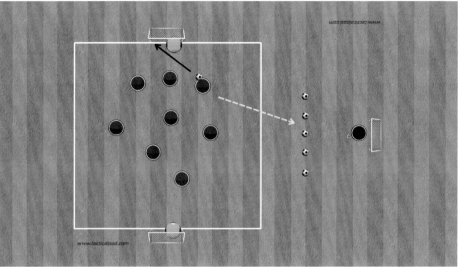

Figure 93. This component brings in the basic concept of a scoreboard, where rewarded players have an opportunity to score an extra point for the team.

ENVIRONMENT

Play a game with the shooting scoreboard described in Tehcnical Game 4 in "The Content" section of this book. When a player scores a goal, they quickly run to the scoreboard and attempt to score past the goalkeeper for a bonus goal. Remember to praise not just the outcome (scoring a goal); use the scoreboard to praise the process too. For example, you may have a player who needs to work on their confidence to shoot or technique for striking the ball. If they create space and display the confidence to shoot and attempt to demonstrate the technique they've been working on, despite perhaps missing the shot, you can praise the process by saying something along the lines of this: "It's excellent that you recognized the opportunity to shoot there! Go to the scoreboard."

BEHAVIORS

As with all scoreboards, I encourage coaches to praise the process. Be on the lookout for positive behaviors and give feedback on the effort displayed, to encourage players to keep investing in their learning. For example, you may have a player who scans the pitch and has recognized the opportunity to pass forward. If they attempt a forward pass that was a good option, but the execution wasn't perfect, and the pass was intercepted, that would still be an opportunity for praise. You could offer this feedback: "Good scanning to recognize that opportunity to play forward. Go to the scoreboard." This praise and reward of the scoreboard will likely encourage the player to continue to scan for passing options, and the execution will improve with time and practice. As the scoreboard's focus is shooting, that may be a behavior you really encourage, promote, and praise in this session.

VARIATIONS

- You can increase or decrease the distance of the shot taken at the scoreboard.

- Figure 93 shows the coach in the scoreboard goal; however, if you're using a goalkeeper, be sure to praise players as much as possible in the game and send them to the scoreboard to keep that goalkeeper busy.

- You can add extra incentive by saying a goal scored at the scoreboard is worth two points.

- A fun progression I've done for the players to further promote best practice when finishing is this: if a player scores their shot at the scoreboard, they can keep shooting until they miss.

- Vary the type of shot, creating a good opportunity to work on free kicks, for example. Maybe add a wall of mannequins if you have the equipment.

COMPONENT 3: DRIBBLE, SHOOT, DEFEND

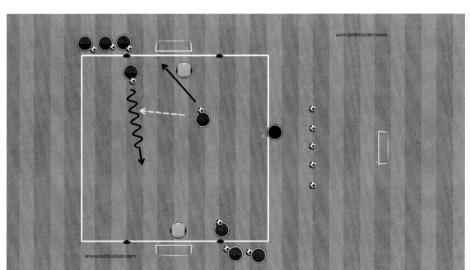

Figure 94. The team that starts the exercise (in this case, red) attempts to score. As soon as the first player shoots, the other team's first player does the same against the other goal, but the red team's shooter becomes an instant defender.

ENVIRONMENT

The first player (in fig. 94, a red-team player) drives in with the ball and tries to score on the goalkeeper. As soon as the player takes the shot, the first player on the other team (in fig. 94, a blue-team player) drives in. The player on the other team who just shot must react to this immediately and become the defender. This pattern repeats, so when this 1v1 dual is over (a goal is scored, the ball goes out of play, or the defender wins the ball), the next red-team player enters. Essentially, players do the following:

- Attack
- Defend
- Rejoin their line and prepare to go again soon

BEHAVIORS

Players should work on running with the ball at speed and attacking space before the defender can recover back, meanwhile ensuring that they don't lose control of the ball, as a heavy touch may give the goalkeeper a chance to go collect the ball. A lot of the problem solving involved in this environment depends on the behaviors of the defender. Are they chasing back at speed, allowing the attacker to cut across the front of the defender to keep them away from the ball? Is the defender closing at an angle and likely to be able to get between the ball and the goal, and therefore, the attacker may look to pretend to shoot before cutting back inside the defender? Practice makes perfect, so the more repetition you can give players on these exercises, the more problem solving they can do, and the more feedback or pointers the coach can provide.

VARIATIONS

- You may progress this to 2v2 with two players entering the field from each team. This can work well by giving the player who shoots or loses the ball a short recovery run (must touch a goal post before they defend, for example).

- Depending on the age or stage of the players, you may work this drill and other games throughout the curriculum with the offside rule in play.

- Be sure to run the drill with players approaching from each side of the goal. So, after a set time, restart the drill by moving the starting point of both groups to the other side of their goal. This will paint a different picture and create different problems for players.

- I like to vary the length or width of the pitch each time I do this practice, to give players different challenges in regard to the time and space they're working with.

COMPONENT 4: GOAL BINGO

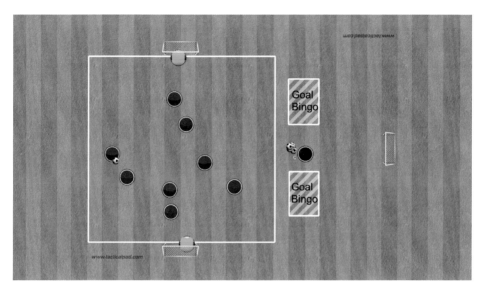

Figure 95. Players have a bingo card to fill up.

ENVIRONMENT

My players love Goal Bingo! But it's important to read the room. Your players may be best suited to finish with a game with no instructions or conditions, or they may want to finish playing the shooting scoreboard from earlier. But Goal Bingo tends to be a favorite, so I hope you can find an appropriate session or time to utilize this game. The players simply play, but both teams have bingo cards at the side of the pitch (printed or handwritten—either works). Each card has the same list of a variety of different ways to score on it. Here's an example:

- First time (a goal scored using one touch to score)

- Left foot (a goal scored with the left foot)

- Right foot (a goal scored with the right foot)

- 3+ passes (a move with three or more passes, ending in a goal)

- Volley (a goal scored by striking a bouncing ball)

Praise bravery of taking a shot and passes or dribbles that lead to goal-scoring opportunities, but you may also praise decision-making regarding when not to shoot. For example, if a player recognizes that a teammate is in a better position and shows disguise, as if they're going to shoot, before passing to that player, that would certainly be a behavior to reward.

VARIATIONS

- There are a lot of different types of goals you might put on the bingo card, such as a rebound, a goal from a certain distance, or a header, depending on the age and stage of the players you're working with.

- Sometimes the bingo card (although fun) can be a bit counterintuitive as players try to score goals that weren't necessarily the best option. Therefore, I've done a variation that has worked well: tell the players that there are two ways to win the game—the first to fill the bingo card or the first to eight goals.

- The coach may have the bingo cards written down and simply keep score for the players, but the younger ones in particular enjoy coming over and marking it off themselves. This creates a momentary overload on the pitch for the team in possession, helping them find a quick solution to goal.

- Play without conditions.

CURRICULUM: Scoreboard Soccer

SESSION: 4

AGE: 8–16

STAGE: Play Football

THEMES: Control, Turning, Long Passing, Awareness, First Touch

COMPONENT 1: CONTROL AND PASS

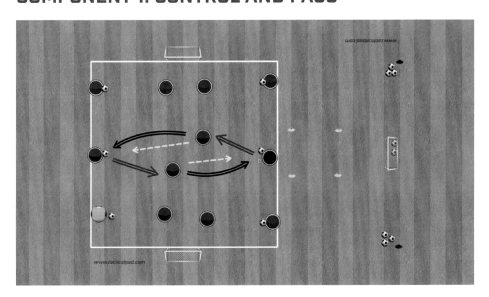

Figure 96. Two players on the outside each pass a ball, at the same time, to a player in the middle, who then controls the ball and makes a long pass in the air to the opposite outside player.

ENVIRONMENT

Figure 96 shows players doing this practice in groups of four; however, you can do it in groups of three by having one person working in the middle or in groups of two by having no one in the middle and players performing longer passes to one another. The practice starts with both players on the outside throwing a ball to a central player, who has checked closer to receive the ball from the air. On receiving the ball, the player looks to get it under control and turn to play a longer pass in the air to the opposite outside player. Once this pass is played, the player follows that ball to receive again and turn to repeat the process. The middle player is always working with the same ball. Players get a point every time an outside player catches their long pass, which will put focus on the height, flight, and accuracy of the pass.

BEHAVIORS

Players should scan before receiving the initial throw to assess their surroundings and then look to cushion the ball with their chest, thigh, or foot to slow the ball down as it drops from the air. Once they have the ball under control, they should look to turn sharply. Advanced players may be able to control and turn into space at the same time before lifting their head again to assess the longer pass. To perform the longer pass, a player should put their head over the ball and kick the bottom of the ball, following through to lift it into the air. The incentive of a point should focus players' attention on trying to kick under and through the ball (like they're trying to cut the grass with their foot) and accurately aiming into the hands of the players on the outside.

VARIATIONS

- Increase or decrease the distance of the longer pass.
- Challenge players on the outside not to catch the ball but to control it with their chest, thigh, or foot.
- Allow the initial throw to be a pass on the ground.

COMPONENT 2: CONTROL PRACTICE

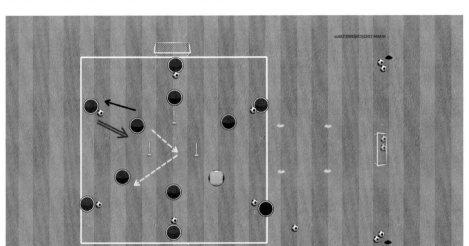

Figure 97. A feeder (red) throws a ball to a player (blue), who then controls the ball and either passes the ball back before moving through the triangle to the next feeder or takes the ball with them.

ENVIRONMENT

This practice involves half of the players becoming feeders on the outside and the other half working on their control from the air. The feeders throw the ball up for a player to control and pass back. After passing back to the feeder, the players travel through the central triangle before moving to a new feeder. You may progress to having the player who controls the ball then turn and dribble through the triangle before passing it to a feeder to start the routine again.

BEHAVIORS

This environment offers opportunities to hone scanning, awareness, decision-making, and control of the ball, with the coach on hand to provide any help or feedback to individual players while the rest of the group keeps practicing. Be sure to rotate the feeders regularly.

VARIATIONS

- Have the feeders work on their throw-in technique by stipulating that the feed must be a throw-in.

- Challenge players by asking feeders to vary their delivery of the ball, such as using a high throw or a bounce pass.

- Give the players in the middle a ball also, which they pass to the feeder as the feeder throws the ball to them to control and turn to go to the next feeder.

COMPONENT 3: CENTRAL TARGET

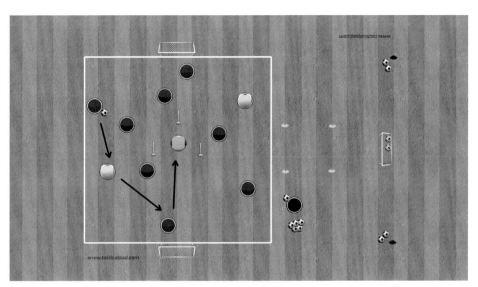

Figure 98. The team in possession must make at least three passes before finding the central player.

ENVIRONMENT

Two teams (plus playmakers) compete in this game, with the aim of passing the ball into a central triangle goal made up of three cones. Before scoring, the team in possession must make a minimum of three passes before trying to find the central player. This encourages players to work on their control while circulating the ball and looking for that final pass that results in a point. Reward this play by asking the central player to play it back to the team who just passed them the ball, rewarding good control, possession, and the final pass, by teams winning the ball back after they score.

BEHAVIORS

The central player can be your goalkeeper, giving them the chance to work on control and playing with their feet. This environment will encourage behaviors such as passing, moving to the surface, and trying to move the ball quickly to create gaps to play into the central area. The team out of possession should be encouraged to stop the split pass into the central area first and foremost, minimizing gaps between players and moving as a unit. The environment also gives coaches a good opportunity to work on the defenders pressing together, winning the ball, and quickly making the pitch big as they transition with a numbers advantage to being the team in possession.

VARIATIONS

- Increase or decrease the area size of both the pitch and the central target area.

- Progress to having the central player as a goalkeeper trying to prevent a driven pass (on the ground) from going through the central area. If they save the ball, they pass it to the other team. If a player scores a goal, play can simply continue as the ball exits the area.

- You may encourage longer passes by saying a controlled long pass is worth two passes, meaning that teams will more quickly reach the target number of passes before scoring by playing longer and working on controlling the ball from the air.

COMPONENT 4: CONTROL SCOREBOARD

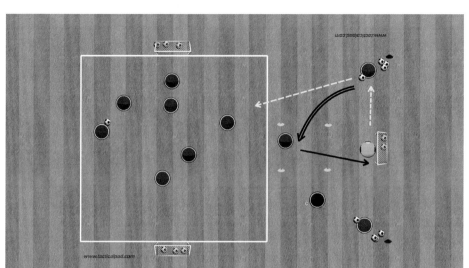

Figure 99. The rewarded player receives a pass from a feeder and attempts to score on the scoreboard goal.

ENVIRONMENT

The scoreboard in this game consists of a six-by-six-yard box, a feeder, a large goal, and a goalkeeper. After scoring a goal in the game, the goal scorer rushes over to the box and receives a pass from the feeder on their team. The gold scorer has one attempt to control the ball within the box and then shoot on goal. If they score, their team receives a bonus goal on top of the current score line from the small-sided game. The shooting player then swaps places with the feeder, who rushes to join the game. Play for a set time limit before resetting the scoreboard to play again. At that point, you may want to mix up the teams or alternate opposition for the players if you have more than one pitch running at the same time.

BEHAVIORS

Be sure to let players know that you'll reward not just goal scoring but also positive behaviors, such as shielding the ball and praising the efforts of teammates, by sending them to the scoreboard. Rewarding such behaviors will motivate players to repeat them. As this scoreboard's focus is control, you might encourage and praise this during the small-sided games. The scoreboard can also give coaches an opportunity to coach control technique on an individual basis.

VARIATIONS

- Vary the length or width of the pitch from session to session to give the players different problems and challenges.

- Increase or decrease the distance of the feed, to support or challenge players.

- Increase or decrease the size of the box players must control the ball in before shooting, to support or challenge players.

- Ask feeders to throw the ball in the air so their teammates can work on control with different parts of the body.

- Rotate the goalkeeper within the game.

- Play to a set number of goals from the scoreboard.

CURRICULUM: Scoreboard Soccer

SESSION: 5

AGE: 8–16

STAGE: Play Football

THEMES: Goalkeeper Distribution, Passing Accuracy, Control, Receiving, Finishing

COMPONENT 1: DISTRIBUTION PRACTICE

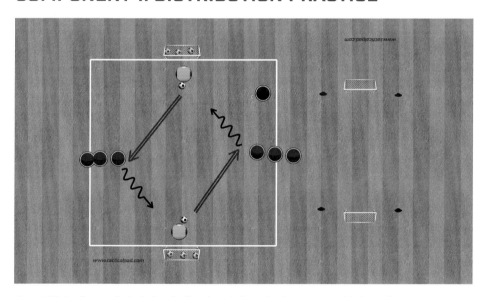

Figure 100. Goalkeepers feed a ball to the first player in line, who then goes 1v1 with the goalkeeper.

ENVIRONMENT

When the coach shouts "go," the goalkeepers feed a ball to the first player in the line on the right-hand side. Upon receiving the ball, they go into a 1v1 situation with the goalkeeper. If the goalkeeper can save and hold the ball, this provides an extra opportunity for the goalkeeper to work on distribution by passing to the attacking player they played the original ball to. Essentially, the game isn't over until both balls end up in the back of the net or off the pitch. Be sure to work the practice to the left also. One progression involves the coach shouting "left" or "right" (instead of "go"), with that being the line the goalkeepers distribute the ball to.

BEHAVIORS

Goalkeeper distribution, 1v1 attacking, and finishing are all part of this competitive practice. This setup will give the goalkeepers an opportunity to practice a variety of ways to distribute the ball—they may use their feet or throw or roll the ball with their hands. Controlling the ball and taking a positive touch toward the goal will be crucial for the attacker, and the environment allows them to improve their finishing when 1v1 with the goalkeeper through practice and repetition. As a coach, you may engage players by asking questions to have them think about decision-making when 1v1 with the goalkeeper. For example, if a player shoots from distance and the goalkeeper easily collects the ball, you may ask the attacker what a better option might be next time.

VARIATIONS

- Make it competitive by keeping scores either as individuals or as a team. To encourage quick play when 1v1 with the goalkeeper, you may stipulate the player to score first gets two goals.

- Play a game of chase. When the attacking player takes their first touch, the player behind them in the line chases them to try to prevent them from scoring. Ensure that players swap roles after each turn.

COMPONENT 2: 1V1 TO GOAL

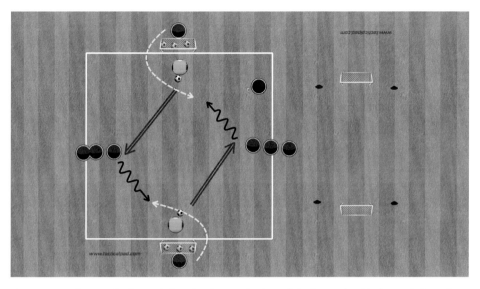

Figure 101. Goalkeepers distribute a ball to the player at the front of the line on the side the coach shouts for. A defender matches up with the attacker.

ENVIRONMENT

The coach shouts "right" or "left" to start the drill. When the coach shouts "right," for example, both goalkeepers distribute a ball to the player at the front of the line on the right-hand side. While this happens, the defender behind the goal also runs to the right (see fig. 101) and comes onto the pitch to defend 1v1 against the player receiving the ball. The attacker looks to get by the defender and score, but if the defender or goalkeeper gets the ball, they immediately start an attack in the other direction. As with component 1, the practice is over only when both balls are no longer in play.

BEHAVIORS

Continue to coach and help goalkeepers with their distribution, attackers with their 1v1 attacking and finishing, and defenders with their 1v1 defending. This environment will ensure that there's a lot of transition for players to work on—for example, defenders or goalkeepers winning the ball and needing to quickly transition into attackers.

VARIATIONS

- Utilize the bonus-ball idea to facilitate some 2v2 games when both initial balls have gone out of play.

- Apply a rotation so all players can work on attacking and defending from both sides. For example, after a player has been the attacker, they can become the defender and, after that, join the line at the other side, continuing to move around the pitch after each rotation.

COMPONENT 3: GOALKEEPER DISTRIBUTION SCOREBOARD

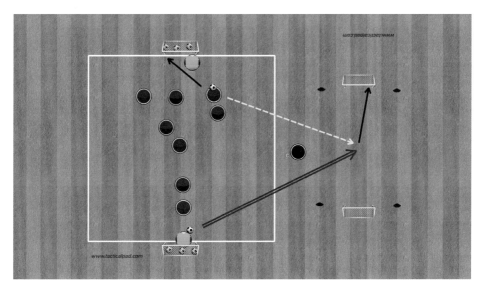

Figure 102. The goalkeeper for the scoring team passes a ball to the goal scorer, who rushes to the scoreboard to attempt at a bonus point.

ENVIRONMENT

A player who scores in the game earns a bonus shot, but they must take the opportunity quickly so they can get back on to help their outnumbered team as soon as possible. Sitting alongside the game, the scoreboard consists of a small pitch with two goals. After a player scores a goal in the game, the goalkeeper of the scoring team quickly grabs a ball from their goal and looks to work on their distribution of the ball by playing a pass to the goal scorer, who rushes to the scoreboard. The goal scorer attempts to quickly receive the ball from the goalkeeper and score a bonus goal on the small pitch. This must all be done with as much pace and quality as possible, as the game resumes immediately, with the opposition trying to take advantage of the momentary overload on the pitch and the briefly distracted goalkeeper, who's working on their distribution. Play first to a set number of goals, totaling the goals from the game and the goalkeeper-distribution challenge.

BEHAVIORS

Be sure to let players know you won't reward just goal scoring but also positive behaviors, such as keeping possession and creating space for others through movement off the ball, by sending them to the scoreboard. Rewarding such behaviors will motivate players to repeat them. As this scoreboard's focus is on goalkeeper distribution, the more you praise outfield players and send them to the scoreboard, the more the goalkeeper gets to react to this and work on their distribution. The scoreboard can also give coaches an opportunity to coach receiving the ball back to goal, turning, and finishing.

VARIATIONS

- Vary the length or width of the pitch from session to session to give the players different problems and challenges.

- Ask, challenge, and coach the goalkeepers to vary their distribution through kicking, throwing, or rolling the ball.

- Rotate the goalkeepers within the game if teams don't have a set goalkeeper and other players want to work on this position.

COMPONENT 4: PLAY A GAME

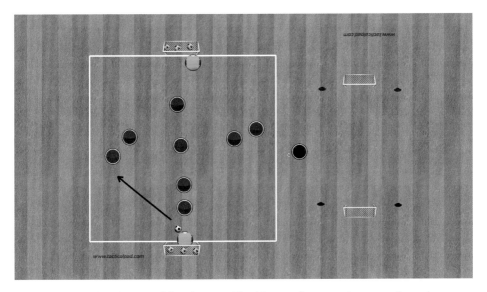

Figure 103. You can introduce a condition where a goal involving a goalkeeper touch counts as five goals.

ENVIRONMENT

Finish on a game of soccer.

Alternatively, you may apply this condition to the game to bring your session focus to the surface: if a player scores a goal that involved the goalkeeper touching the ball, it counts as five goals.

BEHAVIORS

The condition encourages players to have the goalkeeper involved in the buildup play, so they won't hesitate to go back to the goalkeeper when they have the ball and are looking to restart an attack. This will allow the goalkeeper to work on their distribution and look to stay involved in the play.

VARIATIONS

- In the game, instead of the condition described, ask the players if they want to continue the scoreboard idea from component 3.

- Use small-sided games if you have a large number at your session or combine the games to finish on a larger-sided game.

- Play without conditions.

CURRICULUM: Scoreboard Soccer

SESSION: 6

AGE: 8–16

STAGE: Play Football

THEMES: Dribbling, 1v1, Disguised Fitness, Overloads, Underloads

COMPONENT 1: MASTER THE BALL

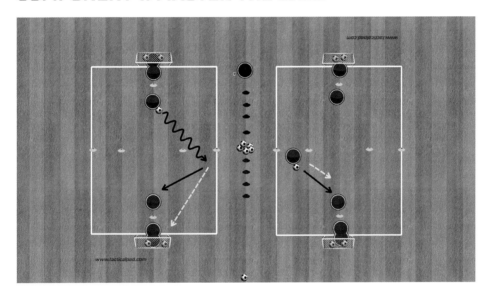

Figure 104. Dribbling practice.

ENVIRONMENT

Set out an area sized appropriately for the age and stage of your players. The setup involves players lined up opposite one another, with two gates halfway between the lines. The player starting with the ball dribbles forward before working on a change of direction and a change of speed to drive through one of the gates. They then pass the ball to the first player in the next line and follow that pass. Repeat the dribbling practice in this fashion. I split the groups into two to maximize the repetition for the players. You can progress this drill by asking the player who passes the ball to the start of the next line to then defend, creating a 1v1 through the gates. If the attacker gets through a gate, the drill continues as normal. If a defender wins the ball, they look to go through the gate and continue the practice.

BEHAVIORS

For attacking 1v1, this environment encourages the development of close control and exaggerated changes of direction accompanied by acceleration to leave the defender behind. For defending 1v1, this environment encourages players' slowing down the attacker, getting their body between the ball and the space they wish to attack, and applying a side-on body position that could force mistakes from the attacker for the defender to then win the ball. Transition is also key in this exercise, as players need to react when winning or losing the ball.

VARIATIONS

- Upon winning the ball, the defender can pass to the next player in the line, to simulate winning the ball and playing a forward pass.

- To allow for more success, you can add a central gate.

- To challenge players further, you can limit the gates to only a wide central gate for players to try and get through.

COMPONENT 2: SWITCH PITCH

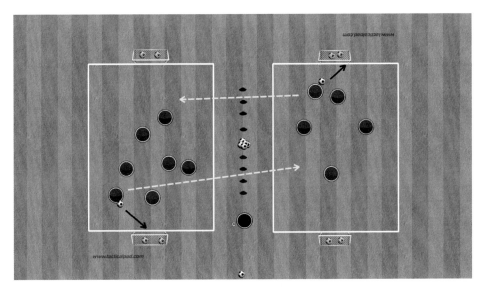

Figure 105. A player who scores joins their team on the other pitch unless they're the last player from their team on the pitch.

ENVIRONMENT

Run two games side by side, and if a player scores, they join your team on the other pitch. The only time they don't move is if they're the last player from their team on a pitch. The first team to ten goals wins. Adapt the number and size of the pitches used to suit the players you're working with.

BEHAVIORS

This game-based environment creates a high level of fun and chaos for the players. Scanning the pitch to constantly assess their surroundings becomes a crucial behavior for players to work on in this environment amid 1v1s, 2v4s, 5v3s, and countless other scenarios. This environment isn't conducive to coaches stopping the games to coach, as while you try to coach on one pitch the scenario might suddenly change due to a goal on the other. My advice is to get the dimensions right, explain the game, and let the players play.

VARIATIONS

- Figure 105 shows the game with two pitches, but you can play with three, four, or more small-sided pitches if you're working with a larger number of players.

- As with most of the games throughout this resource, you can include goalkeepers. If you're not using goalkeepers, mini goals would be ideal.

COMPONENT 3: CONNECT FOUR

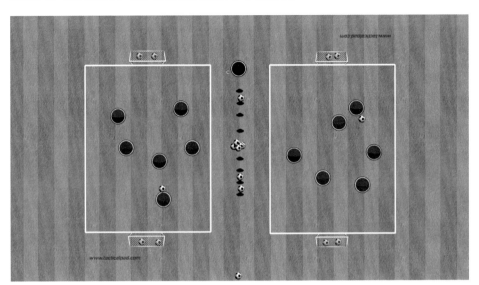

Figure 106. The rewarded player places a ball on one of their team's cones.

ENVIRONMENT

The scoreboard in this game consists of four blue cones and four red cones, with a supply of balls nearby. The blue set of cones represents the blue scoreboard, and the other set, the red. After a player scores or the coach instructs a player to go to the scoreboard due to positive play, the player rushes over to put a ball on one of their team's cones. The first group to fill all four cones wins. This game involves collaboration between the teams wearing the same-color bib, and players will work hard because they know factors on the other pitch might result in them losing the game. At that point, you may choose to reset the scoreboard and add a fun progression where the goal scorer or praised player can either put a ball on their team's cone or kick one off one of the other team's cones.

BEHAVIORS

As always, be sure to let players know that you won't reward just goal scoring but also positive behaviors. Rewarding such behaviors will motivate players to repeat them. Scoreboard Soccer is designed to help in the holistic development of young players through praising and promoting characteristics such as teamwork, sportsmanship, and respect.

VARIATIONS

- If you wish to prolong games, introduce more cones to fill.

- Progress by allowing players to take away a point from the opposition instead of adding one to their scoreboard.

- Promote player autonomy by choosing captains who can praise players on the opposing team by sending them to the scoreboard.

COMPONENT 4: PLAY A GAME

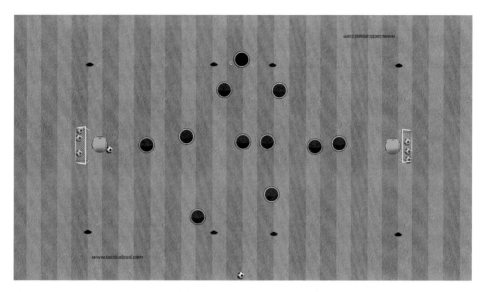

Figure 107. You can bring out the session's focus by adding a condition to an otherwise normal game.

ENVIRONMENT

By simply picking up a couple of cones and moving the goals, you can create a bigger game. Try to minimize setup time and maximize activity throughout all sessions. You might decide to simply let the session finish with a normal game of football and just rotate the goalkeepers frequently. Or you could introduce a condition to bring the focus of the session to the surface. Here's an example condition: if a player scores a goal after dribbling past at least one player, that's worth two goals—a simple condition to encourage players to run with the ball.

BEHAVIORS

This condition will make players mindful of trying to dribble. As coaches, we need to embrace the fact that dribbling and giving the ball away are part of the learning process. Decision-making as to when to dribble will come into play, and coaches can help highlight to young players opportunities to run with the ball and when the best option may be to make a pass. Praising effort as opposed to success is crucial. If players recognize that effort is what's of real value, they'll keep giving this effort and, with time, will be likely to get more success when passing, dribbling, and shooting the ball.

VARIATIONS

- If you have players who play as goalkeepers, they may want to stay in goal for most of the game.

- In the 6v6 game, instead of the condition described, use the Connect Four scoreboard idea.

- Play without conditions.

CURRICULUM: Scoreboard Soccer

SESSION: 7

AGE: 8–16

STAGE: Play Football

THEMES: Possession, Pressing, Awareness, Disguise, Movement Off the Ball

COMPONENT 1: PASSING WARS

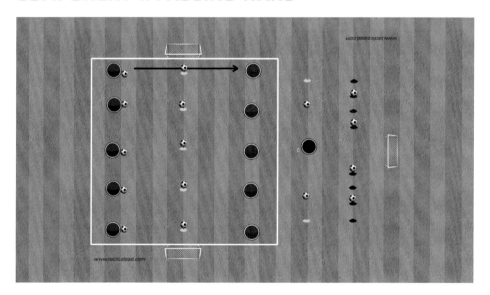

Figure 108. Players compete to be the one who knocks the ball off the cone the most in a set amount of time.

ENVIRONMENT

As with most sessions within this curriculum, this environment setup at the start allows for a smooth journey throughout the entire session. This initial practice involves players passing the ball and attempting to hit a target (a ball on a cone) that's approximately ten yards away. Players play against each other, giving themselves a point when knocking the ball off the cone, before resetting and resuming the game. The player who hits the ball the most during a certain time limit determined by the coach wins.

BEHAVIORS

This is a fun practice to work on the technique of passing the ball on the ground in isolation. Give players space and freedom to problem solve regarding hitting the target, but some may need coaching points. Players are likely to get more success if they use the toes of their standing foot to aim at the target, with their big toes being in line with the front of the ball. They should have a space the size of your standing foot between the aiming and kicking foot, keeping in mind that passes with the inside of the foot tend to be more accurate, striking and following through the center of the ball.

VARIATIONS

- Increase or decrease the distance of the pass by simply asking the players to move back or come closer to the target.

- Encourage players to practice passing with both feet. You might do rounds that are right-foot only and rounds that are left-foot only.

- Progress by adding competition. After each round, the winner of the game moves up a station, and the other player moves down. If a game ends in a draw, you could play it such that the next one to hit the target wins.

COMPONENT 2: TEAM POSSESSION

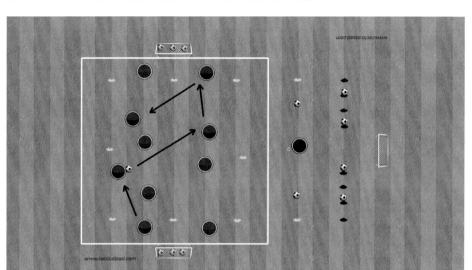

Figure 109. Players use their wall players to keep possession and limit the opposition.

ENVIRONMENT

As a progression from component 1, players now look to pass and keep possession in a 3v3 scenario with a wall player from each team standing at opposite ends on the outside of the area. Figure 109 shows the blue team using their two wall players to keep possession and work the ball from one side of the area to the other, but they can use their wall player at any time to keep the ball. When the red team wins the ball, they then try to keep possession from the blue team and can use the red wall players to do so.

BEHAVIORS

The three players in the middle must look to complement each other to aid possession of the ball. A coaching point I like to make within this exercise is asking the players to think about the central area as four small boxes instead of one big one. Can the three players always look to be in a different area from each other and rotate to get on the ball constantly? This creates angles for the players on and off the ball to find passes and may even open up the pass from wall player to wall player, taking all of the opposition players out of the game with one pass. Scanning, passing, controlling technique, and communication can all be practiced and coached within this environment.

VARIATIONS

- Initially, you can give both teams a ball and make the practice unopposed. Simply look to move the ball among your three players and two wall players with precision and quality while avoiding the traffic of the other team who's doing the same.

- To further support players if needed, you can make all four players on the outside wall players that either team can use.

- To encourage rotations, you can introduce the progression that when a wall player receives the ball they can dribble or pass and follow into the area, with the player who passed the ball to them becoming the wall player.

COMPONENT 3: WALL PLAYER GAME

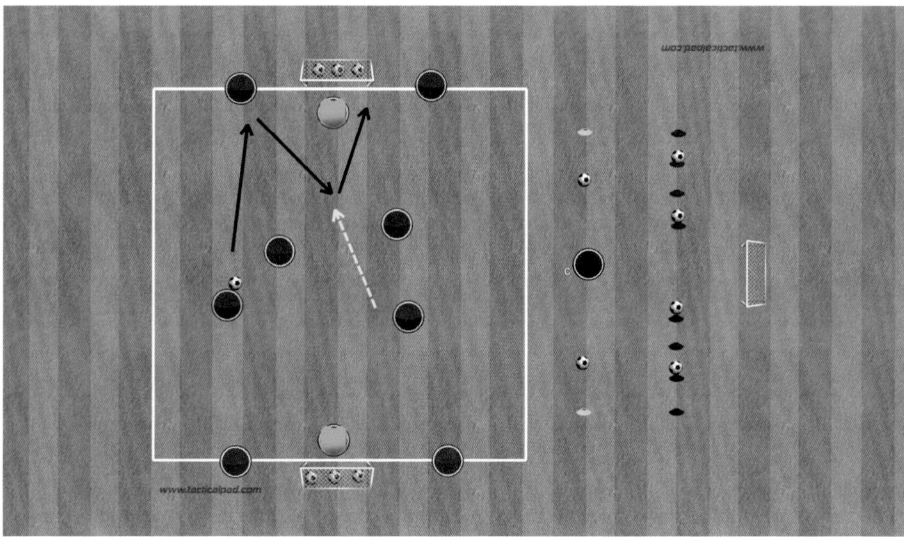

Figure 110. Players play 2v2, using their goalkeeper and wall players to move the ball.

ENVIRONMENT

A player from each team goes in goal. You may choose to rotate the role of the keeper regularly. Each team plays with two players joining the goalkeeper on the pitch and two wall players, who run the line between the opposition's goal and the corner of the pitch. Simply play 2v2, encouraging the team in possession to use both their goalkeeper and two wall players to pass and move the ball in the hope of creating a goal-scoring opportunity. Rotate the players on the pitch with the wall players, using an appropriate work-to-rest ratio for the age and stage of the players you're working with.

BEHAVIORS

Like component 2, the team in possession has a 5v3 overload; however, they're now looking to use this overload to create a chance to score. Through passing and moving, they can look to create chances—for example, players may look to play wall passes with their extra players before scoring or make movements to allow a pass from the goalkeeper to the wall players before then supporting this pass for a layoff and shot on goal. Behaviors to encourage will depend on your own coaching style. Patience in possession to move the defenders away from their goal or tire them out before scoring may be a behavior you want to encourage, or you may use this environment to work on quick forward passes at the earliest opportunity and supporting movements to get on the ball around the opposition's goal.

VARIATIONS

- Encourage possession that will lead to a good chance to score by allowing the goal-scoring team to restart with the ball from their goalkeeper.

- If you want your players to find quick solutions to goal during these attacking overloads, you may set a six- or seven-second time limit on each attack, and if time runs out, the opposition's goalkeeper starts with the ball. This may focus the defenders on working on delaying attacks.

- Make the games competitive by implementing a winner-stays-on system.

COMPONENT 4: COCONUT SHY SCOREBOARD GAME

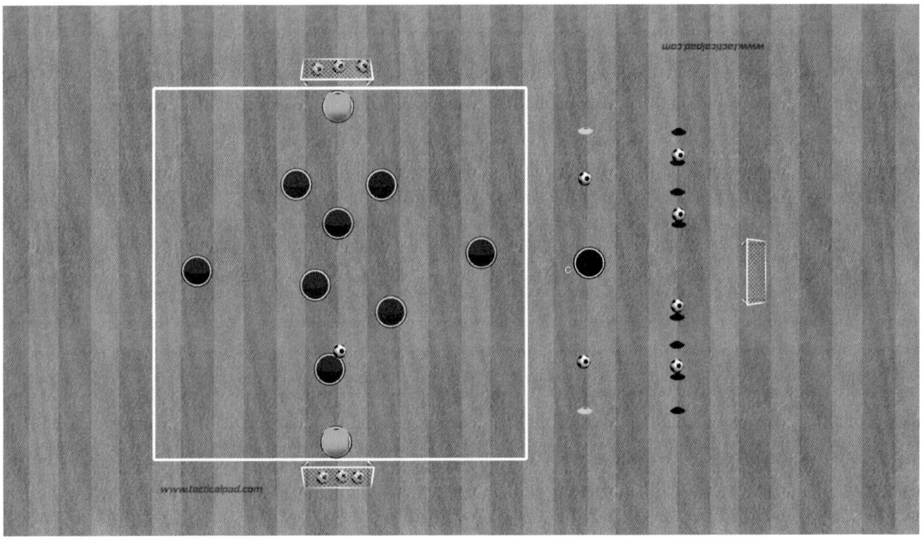

Figure 111. The rewarded player attempts to empty one of their cones. If successful, they add the ball to one of the opposition's cones.

ENVIRONMENT

When a player scores a goal, the conceding team collects the ball and immediately continues the game while the goal scorer quickly goes to the scoreboard. In this scoreboard, each team has a set of four cones, with balls on top of two. The team's aim is to empty their four cones and fill the other team's. The first to do so wins. From a distance appropriate for the age and stage of players you're working with, the rewarded player has one pass to try and knock a ball off one of their cones. If successful, they then add this ball to the other one of the other team's cones. If unsuccessful, they put back the ball they passed back and rejoin the game.

BEHAVIORS

As with all scoreboard games, the rewarded player should try to get a point via the scoreboard as quickly as possible to get back on the pitch to help their teammates, who are currently playing a player short. This increases the opposition's chance of scoring a goal or demonstrating positive play to be sent to the scoreboard.

VARIATIONS

- As with all scoreboard games, the number of players involved in the games can be easily adapted depending on how many players you're working with.

- Vary the length or width of the pitch from session to session to give the players different problems and challenges.

- Increase the number of cones and balls to knock off, to prolong the game.

- Increase or decrease the length of the pass to knock a ball off the cone at the scoreboard.

CURRICULUM: Scoreboard Soccer

SESSION: 8

AGE: 8–16

STAGE: Play Football

THEMES: Dribbling, 1v1, Turning, Awareness, Panenka

COMPONENT 1: MOVING WITH THE BALL

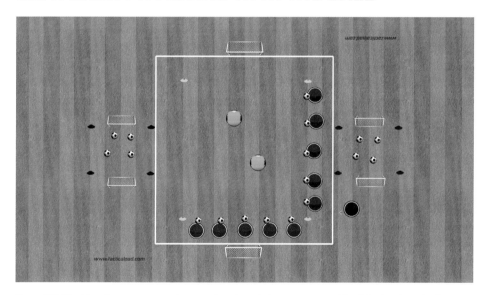

Figure 112. The blue players run across the area, then the red players run across. The defenders (green) offer a progression, testing the other players' close control.

ENVIRONMENT

Figure 112 shows an environment that includes the pitch and goals for scoreboard games throughout this session, but for component 1, all you need is a twenty-by-twenty-yard area with half the players working horizontally (in fig. 112, the blues) and the other half working vertically (in fig. 112, the reds). The players along the side of the pitch start by running across the area, and when they reach the other side, the players along the end of the pitch go. When they reach the other end of the pitch, the team along the side runs across again. This simple environment repeats to allow players a lot of repetition regarding running with the ball. The two green defenders in figure 112 show a simple progression to test players' close control.

BEHAVIORS

I've used this to give players freedom and allow them to practice their dribbling technique, but I've also used this setup to work on specific close-control techniques. For example, you might challenge players to get as many touches as they can while going across the box at a steady pace and try to get more touches each time. This stresses the behavior of ball mastery. Alternatively, you can have them see how quickly they can get across the box, which would involve bigger touches and strides to attack space.

VARIATIONS

- Add or reduce the number of defenders in the middle. You can implement a rotation where if the defender wins a ball the player they won it from becomes the defender.

- Encourage use of both feet. You might establish that on the first pass players use their right foot, and on the way back, they use their left, with this repeating throughout the practice.

- Prior to adding defenders, you can use this setup to work on different ball-manipulation moves across the box—for example, toe taps.

COMPONENT 2: INDIANA JONES SCOREBOARD GAME

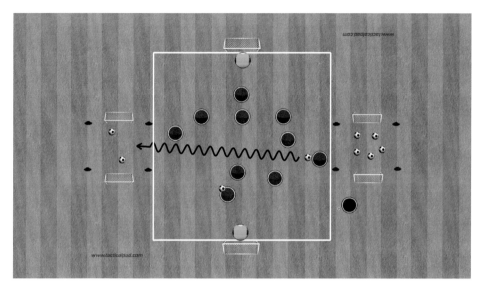

Figure 113. A rewarded player dribbles a ball from the other team's scoreboard across the pitch to their team's scoreboard.

ENVIRONMENT

This game has two scoreboards, one for each team, and the aim is for teams to have the most balls in their scoreboard by the end of the game, or you can play such that the first to get all balls wins. As figure 113 shows, the goal scorer or praised player takes a ball from the other team's scoreboard and dribbles across the pitch to put it in theirs. As with all scoreboard games, the game always continues; therefore, the challenge is for the rewarded player to be able to dribble through a live game to give their team a point. This is a great scoreboard to really encourage and embrace dribbling the ball; therefore, that might be something to reward during the game.

BEHAVIORS

This scoreboard also challenges the other players, those within the game, regarding scanning and awareness, looking out for any players dribbling across the pitch as the game is played. Be sure that you deliver this with the element of the health and safety of your players in mind; if you don't feel that the players are controlled and sensible enough for this environment, add a condition that the ball must stay below waist height during the game or don't use this game.

VARIATIONS

- Vary the length or width of the pitch from session to session to give the players different problems and challenges.

- Increase the distance between scoreboards to ensure even more running with the ball.

- Players within the game can't interfere with the player dribbling across to add to their scoreboard. But if you're working with more-experience players, you can add a progression that allows them to try to stop the player from getting across the pitch.

- Again, always be mindful of the maturity and ability of your players and use scoreboard games appropriate for the players' age and stage to ensure that games are played safely.

COMPONENT 3: ZONE SOCCER

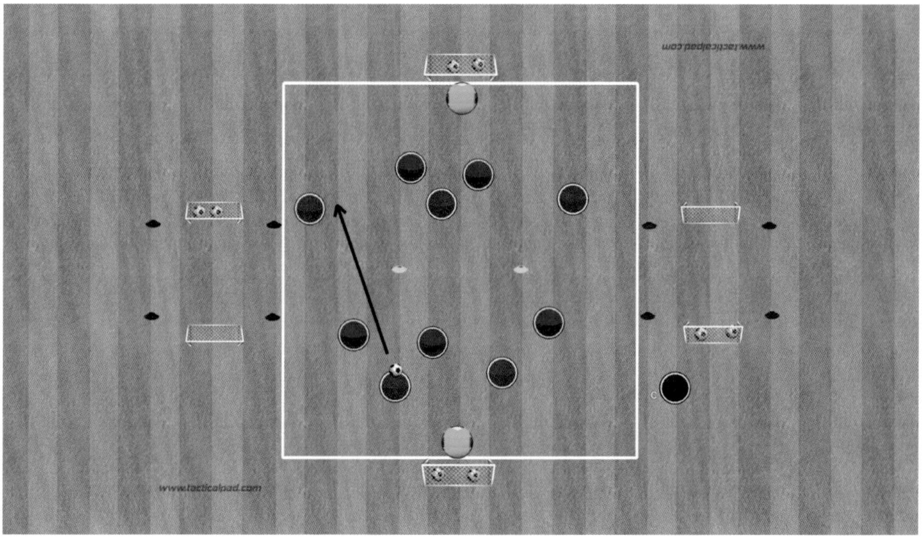

Figure 114. Players must play on their side of the halfway line.

ENVIRONMENT

This practice is a 5v5 game with goalkeepers and a halfway line. Assign each player to a half of the pitch to play the game in. As figure 114 shows, each team has two defenders in one half and three attackers in the other.

BEHAVIORS

This environment allows attackers to work in 3v2 situations and defenders to work on defending in 2v3 situations. I discuss these scenarios in more detail in "The Coaching" section of this book, and some of the things I discuss there may help coaches facilitate learning in this environment. A behavior you can work to develop in this exercise is defenders playing out from the back. Since they're under pressure from three attackers, it's crucial that they utilize the goalkeeper as an extra player and also look to receive in a manner that will allow them to play forward as quickly and accurately as possible. Holding on to the ball too long may result in a turnover of possession near a team's own goal.

VARIATIONS

- Allow one striker to drop deep to get the ball. From there, the player may turn and dribble over the half and start an attack, or their movement may allow a pass from the goalkeeper or defenders straight into one of their teammates, and they can turn and support that pass.

- Allow a defender to dribble over the halfway line and join the attack.

- When the ball passes the halfway line, allow a member from the team who isn't in possession to recover back and help the two defenders.

- Progress to removing the halfway line and simply playing an all-in game.

COMPONENT 4: PANENKA SCOREBOARD GAME

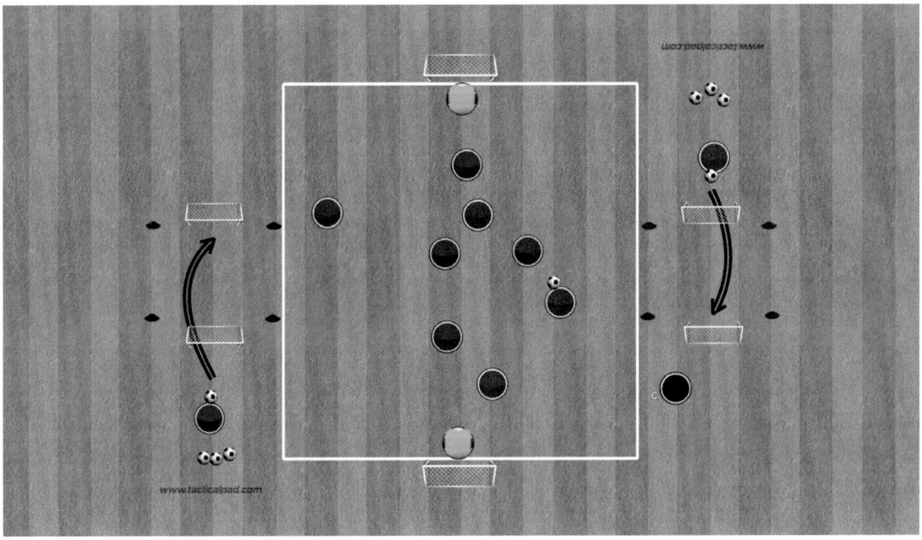

Figure 115. The rewarded player attempts to loft a ball over one goal and into the next.

ENVIRONMENT

The scoreboard in this game consists of a supply of balls and two small goals, with one placed five yards behind the other. After scoring a goal in the game, the goal scorer rushes to the scoreboard and attempts to loft the ball over the first small goal and have it land in the second for a point. Play for a set time limit, and the team with the most combined goals from the game and the scoreboard wins. Then reset the scoreboard to play again. At that point, you may want to mix up the teams or alternate opposition for the players if you have more than one pitch running at the same time.

BEHAVIORS

Be sure to let players know that you won't reward just goal scoring but also positive behaviors, such as a good first touch of the ball and never giving up, by sending them to the scoreboard. Rewarding such behaviors will motivate players to repeat them. As this scoreboard's focus is the Panenka technique of lofting the ball in a disguised fashion, you can encourage and praise this during the small-sided games. The scoreboard can also give coaches an opportunity to coach the Panenka on an individual basis.

VARIATIONS

- Vary the length or width of the pitch from session to session to give the players different problems and challenges.

- Increase or decrease the distance to and between the mini goals.

- Implement a scoring system of one point for a successful Panenka that finishes in the back goal but five points if it goes in the goal without bouncing first.

CURRICULUM: Scoreboard Soccer

SESSION: 9

AGE: 8–16

STAGE: Play Football

THEMES: Passing, Defending, Transition, Finishing Goalkeeping

COMPONENT 1: PLAY A GAME

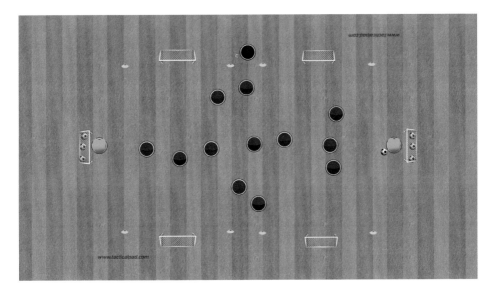

Figure 116. This session involves a normal game but set up the area for the remainder of the session.

ENVIRONMENT

Start by playing a game of football. The area can be adapted depending on how many players you're working with. In preparation for the remainder of the session, I set goals for smaller-sided games. For all components and sessions, if you don't have goals or cones, bibs for goalposts are fine. This component involves letting the players just play a game, something I think is crucial as part of longer-term development, facilitating plenty of game time with freedom of movement and encouraging players to express themselves.

BEHAVIORS

The nature of a game of football should allow players plenty of opportunities to pass, dribble, shoot, and practice behaviors such as teamwork, communication, and resilience.

VARIATIONS

- Play smaller-sided games.

- Play larger-sided games, depending on your numbers.

- Use player-led games, asking the players if they want to play 4v4 or 8v8, for example.

COMPONENT 2: SMALL-SIDED GAMES

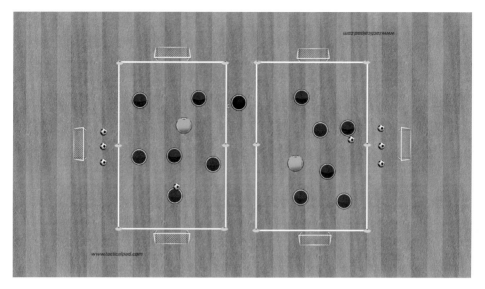

Figure 117. This component involves a large-sided game, a small-sided game, a four-goal game, and another large-sided game.

ENVIRONMENT

This session is very much a game-based session. Starting with a large-sided game, moving into small-sided games, then a four-goal game, and finishing on another large-sided game. I can't overstate how often I do game-based sessions with players of this age and stage and how much they enjoy them, which for me, is the most important thing.

BEHAVIORS

I like playing games with a playmaker. As figure 117 shows, in these games, it's 3v3 with a playmaker who plays for the team in possession. This gives great opportunities for players to work on decision-making when in possession of the ball, pushing them to think, Are all my teammates being covered by the opposition defenders? In that case, they need to think, I may be able to travel with the ball. Has my ball carrying brought a defender toward me? If so, can I scan the pitch to find the open player? Does the extra player give me an opportunity for a wall pass? Or I may even use them as a decoy wall pass before dribbling. There's lots of repetition of decision-making and technical skills within these environments. The playmaker will also test teams out of possession to defend outnumbered, and some of the fundamental coaching points from "The Coaching" section may be useful here.

VARIATION

- Play small-sided games utilizing a scoreboard. As figure 117 shows, I set up a crossbar challenge scoreboard, should the players want to play that. Having a scoreboard to fall back on can be a great idea if players need extra motivation. You might identify some players in the games who aren't getting involved enough. Utilizing a scoreboard game can help you praise and encourage greater involvement in the game from these players.

COMPONENT 3: FOUR-GOAL GAME

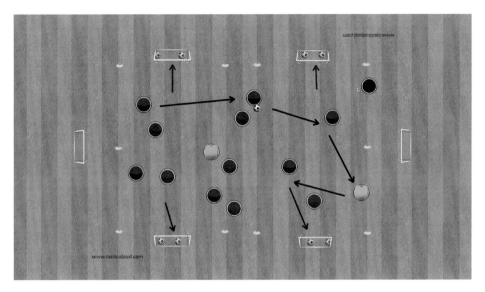

Figure 118. The blue team attacks the goals pointed to by the blue arrows, and the red team attacks the goals pointed to by the red arrows.

ENVIRONMENT

Join the two small pitches together to create a 6v6+2 playmakers. One team (in fig. 118, the blue team) attacks both goals on one side (in fig. 118, marked by blue arrows), and the other team attacks both goals on the other side (in fig. 118, marked by red arrows). The green playmakers shown in figure 118 help the team in possession. Once the game has started, you can pick up the yellow cones that previously separated the two pitches.

BEHAVIORS

Spreading out to utilize space and support fluid transition should help the team in possession keep the ball. Crowding each other's space and bringing pressure to the ball will negate the advantage of having the extra players. Ball possession and switching play to create space to pass forward (into a mini goal) are behaviors I encourage for the team with the ball in this environment. For the team without the ball, defending compact and being between the ball and the goals are key factors. Other key factors include minimizing spaces between players and shifting as the ball moves, to defend the mini goals. If the defending team can implement a solid defense block and shift to protect both goals, it may then give you an opportunity to highlight some defensive triggers for trying to win the ball, such as a bad touch or an under-hit pass. On a turnover of possession, transition becomes crucial for both teams, as I mention in "The Coaching" section of this book.

VARIATIONS

- An alternative exercise in this environment is to play 6v6+2 (with the additional number being flexible depending on the number of players you have), and once the team in possession makes ten passes, they can score in any of the four mini goals.

- To further support the attackers and challenge the defenders, you might make it a six-goal game. The yellow cones shown in figure 118 could become another goal. This may be something you need to apply during the practice, depending on how it's going.

- Four-goal games provide a fun environment to work on goalkeepers. Have a goalkeeper defending two goals, which would give them an opportunity to work on moving their feet quickly and often diving to save shots.

COMPONENT 4: PLAY A GAME

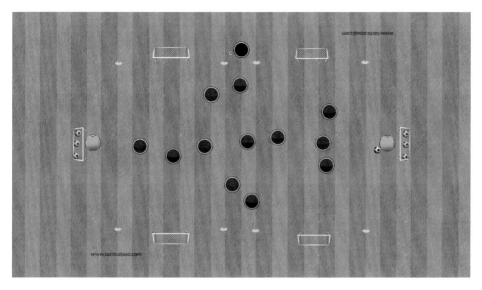

Figure 119. Players finish this session with a large-sided game.

ENVIRONMENT

This component is a game of soccer with no instruction or conditions. As mentioned, this session is a game-based session, starting with a large-sided game, moving into small-sided games, then a four-goal game, and finishing on this large-sided game.

BEHAVIORS

You may choose to coach or speak to players on an individual basis to provide feedback or support during the game. Players tend to engage better and benefit most from one-to-one conversations, and this can be done while the rest of the players play the game and enjoy all the benefits of a game-based approach to training.

VARIATION

- Again, I encourage playing a lot of soccer during this stage of a player's development. Another tool I often use during games is scenario-based training—for example, telling the players, "It's the last ten minutes of the World Cup Final, and the blue team is two goals ahead. Play!" You may try this approach for your players to work on a variety of scenarios in training that are similar to what they may face in a game.

CURRICULUM: Scoreboard Soccer

SESSION: 10

AGE: 8 – 16

STAGE: Play Football

THEMES: Crossing, Finishing, Defending, Dribbling, Transition

COMPONENT 1: DRIBBLE AND DELIVER

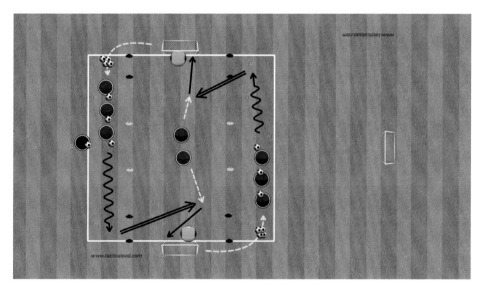

Figure 120. The first player on each team dribbles down the channel and delivers to the central player, who shoots the ball.

ENVIRONMENT

Adapt area sizes depending on the age, stage, and number of players you're working with. Don't hesitate to adapt area sizes during components if what you have isn't working. In this component, players work on crossing and finishing from a wide area. The first player from each team starts with a ball at the same time. They dribble down the channel and deliver to the central player, who shoots the ball. The rotation is simple, with the dribbling player getting ready to shoot next and the next player in the line starting to dribble. After a player's shot, they collect their ball and join the next line, as the curved yellow arrows in figure 120 show.

BEHAVIORS

Driving with the ball at pace to get down the channel is crucial, but players must scan the central area to see where they're going to deliver the ball and deliver with composure, precision, and pace. Communication is key for the crossing and central players to build a relationship. The central player shouldn't minimize the space for the ball to be played into by arriving near the goal too early. Staying farther out and communicating where they want the ball will help them to attack that space with pace and meet the ball from behind to generate power on the strike of the ball.

VARIATIONS

- Be sure to run this practice down both sides. After working on the cross coming from the right, rearrange the players so the ball then comes from the left.

- You may want to include the goalkeepers in the rotation—cross, shoot, become the goalkeeper, then join the line.

- You may want to stagger the exercise to incorporate a defender. So, after the red player shoots, for example, the blue players immediately start while the red player recovers to try and defend their attempt. This would result in the practice working as follows: cross, shoot, defend, then rejoin your own team's line.

- Add competition to focus players on the quality of their delivery of the ball and finishing. For example, play such that the first player to ten points wins, with one point for an assist and two points for a goal.

COMPONENT 2: FINAL BALL

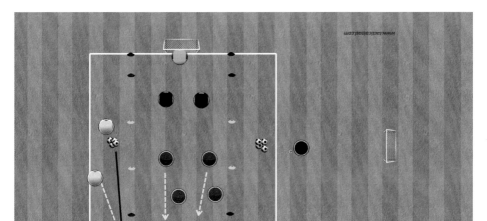

Figure 121. Here, the white team is the first to work on their crossing. A repeated rotation continues.

ENVIRONMENT

The players now work in teams of two. In figure 121, the first team to work on their crossing is the white team. They take turns crossing for the central teams. This continuous practice works as represented in figure 121:

The blue team attacks the red team in an attempt to score from the cross. When this attack is over, the blue team stays to defend the goal they just attacked, and the red team moves up the pitch to attack the black team while attempting to score from the next cross (again always coming from the white team). The red team stays to defend the goal they just attacked as the black team goes to attack the blue team, while attempting to score from the next cross. The practice continues in this fashion, with teams in the middle essentially following this order of actions:

- Attack
- Rest
- Defend
- Repeat

BEHAVIORS

- Allow the defenders to press and try to win the ball from the white team's player. This means there may be a 2v1 for the white team's player to create space and deliver to.

- Allow the white team's player to drive into the central area with the ball, essentially creating a 3v2 to goal. If the defender presses them, can they deliver to the free player? If the defenders continue to mark 2v2 in the middle, can the white team's player drive to goal?

VARIATIONS

- Rotate the crossing players frequently.

- If a team scores from their attack, allow them to go up the other side and attack again. Essentially, one team stays as the attacking team until they miss. Players see which team can score the most in a row.

- Allow the defenders to press and try to win the ball from the white team's player. This means that there may be a 2v1 for the white team's player to create space and deliver to.

- Allow the white team's player to drive into the central area with the ball, essentially creating a 3v2 to goal. If the defender presses them, can they deliver to the free player? If the defenders continue to mark 2v2 in the middle, can the white team's player drive to goal?

COMPONENT 3: WIDE SUPPORT

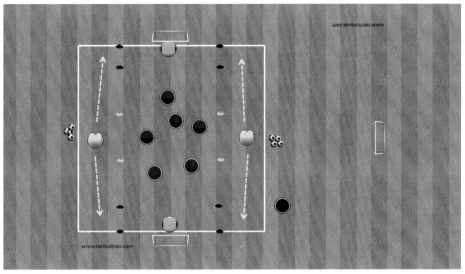

Figure 122. Playmakers must stay in the channels.

ENVIRONMENT

This practice is a 3v3 game with goalkeepers, and the pitch is adapted to have two channels at each side of the pitch (consistent from the setup of components 1 and 2). Operating in each channel are playmakers, who play for the team in possession. Teams can utilize the playmakers at any time, and players from both the team in possession and the team out of possession may enter the channels; however, the playmakers must stay and play in these areas.

BEHAVIORS

The overloads in wide areas should allow teams to get the ball into these areas, which can help in a variety of ways. It can help keep the ball and work it side to side. This is useful if the opposition is compact and well organized regarding defending their goal. Switching the play to the extra players can attract the opposition away from their goal. Another advantage to using the wide players is being able to work on crossing and finishing techniques and movements practiced throughout the session. The wide players may cross from deep, dribble down the channels to deliver, or look to pass down the channel to a teammate who's moved into this area.

VARIATIONS

- If the players you're working with are at an age and stage that involves playing with an offside line, you can introduce the offside rule into this and other games.

- Tell the wide players that if they wish to enter the central area they can do so but only through a blue or red gate. This brings the theme from the practices into a game situation.

- Add the progression that when a playmaker is crossing, the playmaker on the opposite side can enter the pitch to attack the cross.

- Another game you can play with this setup is the playmakers simply start in the channels, but when a team passes the ball to a playmaker, the playmaker can choose to dribble or pass and follow into the central area. This makes it so playing wide can ultimately unlock two extra players for a team. On a turnover of possession, the playmakers must quickly return to the wide channels for the next phase of play.

COMPONENT 4: CROSSING SCOREBOARD GAME

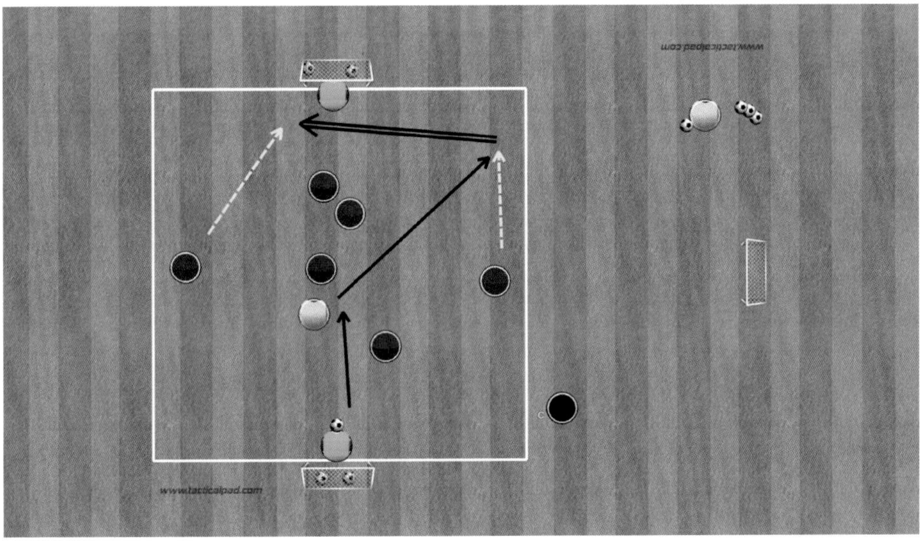

Figure 123. A player working on crossing delivers the ball, angled away from a goal.

ENVIRONMENT

The scoreboard in this game consists of having a player whom the coach has allocated to work on their crossing, delivering the ball from an appropriate distance, angled away from a goal. After scoring a goal in the 3v3+1 game, the goal scorer rushes to receive a cross from the crossing player. If they score from the cross, that goal can be added to the score within the game. It's at the coach's discretion as to if the quality of the goal from the cross is worth a bonus goal. For example, you might stipulate that the ball can only bounce once before a player strikes it or can't bounce at all.

BEHAVIORS

Be sure to let players know that you'll send them to the scoreboard for a variety of reasons, not just goal scoring but also any display of positive play in relation to the player's ability level. Positive behaviors such as foot skills and determination may result in the coach rewarding individuals by sending them to the scoreboard. Rewarding such behaviors will motivate players to repeat them. As this scoreboard's focus is crossing, you might encourage and praise this during the small-sided games. The scoreboard can also give coaches an opportunity to coach crossing on an individual basis.

VARIATIONS

- Swap the crossing player frequently.

- Swap the playmaker frequently.

- Vary the size, distance, and angle to work on different crosses.

- Add a defender or goalkeeper (or both) to help defend the cross, to further challenge the crossing player and the attacker seeking a bonus goal.

THE CURRICULUM

STRATEGY SOCCER

Develops players' knowledge and implementation of more-intricate parts of the game, such as team strategy and style of play.

STRATEGY SOCCER—INTRODUCTORY EXERCISE

In regard to the Strategy Soccer curriculum that follows, I recommend beginning each session with a thorough warm-up. A pre-session warm-up helps prepare the muscles for exercise and reduce the risk of injury, while preparing players mentally for the session ahead. Figure 124 shows an example warm-up with players starting in lines and running to the the yellow cones and back. I'd incorporate repetitions of the following into this warm-up:

- Jogging

- Side steps

- High knees

- Heel kicks

- Skipping

- Backward jogging

- Jumping, landing, and moving

I recommend following up this physical warm-up with some dynamic stretches:

- Quad stretches

- Hamstring stretches

- Knee pulls

- Leg swings

- Squats

- Lunges

You may have players who are experienced and knowledgeable enough to lead their own warm-up. I recommend further reading and research to ensure that you or a fellow coach can provide players with a suitable warm-up before starting the exercises within your session. After the warm-up or dynamic stretching, I encourage my players to do rondos as final preparation for the session ahead.

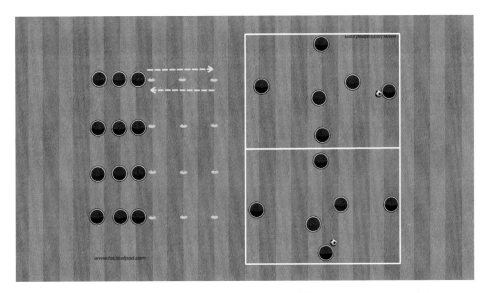

Figure 124. Having a set warm-up can give players routine and responsibility if you ask them to lead it themselves.

CURRICULUM: Strategy Soccer

SESSION: 1

AGE: 12+

STAGE: Learn Football

THEMES: Passing, Possession, Switching Play, Awareness, Movement Off the Ball, Transition

COMPONENT 1: TRANSITION RONDO

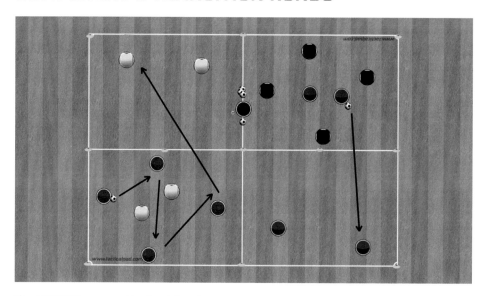

Figure 125/ This component involves 4v2 rondos.

ENVIRONMENT

The session 1, component 1 setup involves the same exercise being duplicated on each side of the pitch and each being carried out in an area with a halfway line creating two boxes. As an example, figure 125 shows the red and white teams' players doing a 4v2 rondo in one box, with the other two players from the defending (white) team taking up positions in another box. The red team gets a point by completing sixteen passes before making a final successful pass to the two defending players in the other box. This creates a turnover of possession, requiring all white-team players to transfer quickly to the box the ball is now in, in an attempt to keep the ball for sixteen passes and get a point themselves. Two red players must then press the ball and try to prevent the white team from getting a point. The process continues in this fashion. If the defenders win the ball before they opposition make sixteen passes, the defenders pass it up to their teammates and restart the exercise with possession of the ball. If the ball goes out of play, the other team starts with the ball.

BEHAVIORS

When in possession of the ball, 4v2 players should try to utilize the space as best as they can, spreading out and constantly moving their feet to show for the ball, therefore making it difficult for the two defenders to track the ball down. Weight of pass, communication, and awareness are all behaviors that will surface the more often players are put into rondo environments. The defenders should look to recognize moments to press or intercept the ball with determination. The 4v2 scenario also gives the two defenders plenty of opportunities to create a press that will dilute the 4v2 to a 2v2. Can the closest defender press the ball in such a way as to show the attacker only one possible pass? This would mean that the second defender could be ready to press the receiving player as the ball travels. Transition is a crucial aspect for the team that makes sixteen passes, passes forward, and then must press. This situation artificially creates a situation where the team that tries to pass forward and loses the ball must instantly press. Transition is also crucial if the defenders win the ball and must immediately play forward out of pressure before supporting that pass.

VARIATIONS

- Increase or decrease the area size to challenge or support players.

- Limit the number of touches attackers can take within the rondo.

- You may have to adjust the number of players in the rondo depending on how many players you have. It may be 5v2 rondos or even using a playmaker who can always play for the team with the ball and transition between each side of the box as the ball does.

COMPONENT 2: FOUR TEAM RONDO

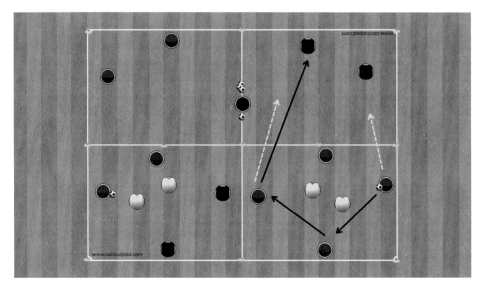

Figure 126. This component involves four-team rondos as a progression of the previous component.

ENVIRONMENT

Session 1, component 2 is a progression from component 1, using the same area; however, figure 126 shows that how teams are created differently. (You shouldn't have to change any bibs from component 1. Just move players.) Following the right-hand side of the diagram, the 4v2 rondo consists of the blue and red teams working together to keep the ball from the white team. After a minimum of four passes, either a red- or a blue-team player passes the ball forward to the black team. If a blue player makes this pass, both blue-team players transition with the ball to the other box. The white team will still be chasing the ball and, therefore, will also follow the ball to the other box, creating a 4v2 with the blue team and the black team, keeping the ball from the white team and trying to transfer back to the red team after a minimum of four passes. On winning the ball, the white team would play to the team in the other box and join them as the team who lost the ball chases to become the defending team.

BEHAVIORS

Communication and support play from the team who passes forward becomes really important in this exercise, players letting the team who's receiving the ball know they're coming to provide support and creating good angles and distances to help keep the ball in the new 4v2 rondo. It's important for the two players in the other box to be giving good length for the longer pass into the next box. Being too close to the play will likely not give players enough time to support the ball, and the defenders will be able to cover ground quicker to win the ball. The two players who are looking for the longer pass should constantly be providing length and moving to create forward passing angles for the player on the ball in the 4v2 rondo. Pressing and quick transition are key behaviors for the defenders to be working on within this environment.

VARIATIONS

- Increase or decrease the area size to challenge or support players.

- Vary the number of touches the team in possession has or the number of passes they need to make before the ball is transitioned.

- This 4v2+2 transition rondo could easily be adapted into a 6v3+3 rondo if you have more players.

COMPONENT 3: 4V4 + 8 GAME

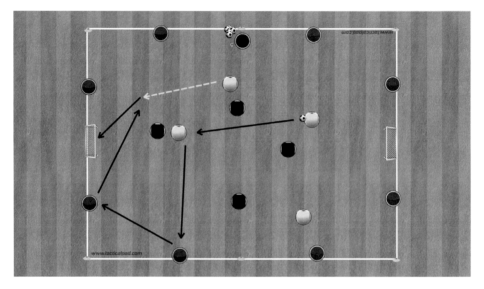

Figure 127. To win, the team in possession can either complete forty passes in a row or score a goal.

ENVIRONMENT

Players now work on keeping possession over larger distances. As figure 127 shows, the environment is four players in white against four players in black. Each team can use the wall players around the outside of the pitch; wall players, however, can pass to each other a maximum of one time in a row. To win the game, the team in possession can either complete forty passes in a row or score a goal. If the black team loses, they switch with the blue team, and if the blue team loses, they switch with the black team for the next game. If the white team loses, they switch with the red team, and if the red team loses, they switch with the white team for the next game.

BEHAVIORS

This environment allows for plenty of practice in regard to decision-making and keeping the ball. Utilizing the wall players and supporting teammates by giving good angles and quality passes should allow the team in possession to keep the ball. The crucial decision for teams to make is whether to build up toward forty passes to win the game or to recognize that during the buildup they have created gaps in the other team to exploit and go for goal. The four defenders need to recognize how difficult it'll be to chase the ball and cover twelve opposition players. This environment can allow you to work on the four moving as a unit to minimize a threat on the goal and start to create traps for where they want the opposition to pass the ball before being in a situation to try to win the ball from the players they've isolated.

VARIATIONS

- Increase or decrease the area size to challenge or support players.

- You might stipulate that the wall players need to play using only one or two touches each time the ball comes to them.

COMPONENT 4: PASSES EQUAL POINTS

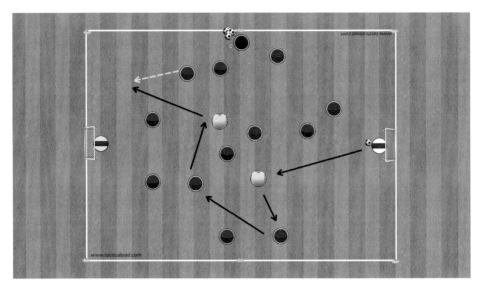

Figure 128. Goals are valued by the number of passes leading to the goal.

ENVIRONMENT

Using the same area size as component 3 (as always, try to plan sessions for a smooth transition between components), create two teams and implement an overload by having one or two playmakers play for the team in possession. Simply play a game of football; however, value goals at the number of passes leading to the goal. For example, if a team plays five passes and then scores, they get five points. This encourages possession of the ball, as worked on throughout the session,

BEHAVIORS

The incentive of passes being worth goals really focuses the players regarding keeping possession of the ball. Crucially, it also helps players work on decision-making. If a team has accumulated ten passes, players will start to value the buildup play and not want it to go to waste. They'll be very focused on finishing the move, with a goal that will hone decision-making skills in front of the goal.

VARIATIONS

- Increase or decrease the area size to challenge or support players.
- Play without conditions or instructions.

CURRICULUM: Strategy Soccer

SESSION: 2

AGE: 12+

STAGE: Learn Football

THEMES: Defending, 2v2, Concentration, Communication, Tackling, Implementing a Game Plan

COMPONENT 1: 2V2 DEFENDING

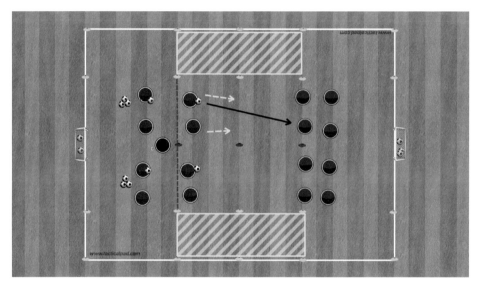

Figure 129. The blue team (attacking) can use the yellow zones anytime, but the red team (defending) can use them only if the ball is in there. The blue team must dribble past the line created by the final red and yellow cones.

ENVIRONMENT

As with a variety of activities throughout this book, this exercise replicates to maximize repetition for the players. In 2v2 channels (in fig. 129, between the line of red and yellow cones), players play 2v2, starting with the red team passing to the blue team before defending them 2v2. For a point, the blue team must get past the final red or yellow cone, represented by dotted red lines in figure 129. The blue team can use the yellow highlighted zone, but the red team is allowed to enter this zone only if the ball is in there. Despite the blue team being allowed to use the yellow zone, reiterate that they must dribble past the line created by the final red and yellow cones.

BEHAVIORS

You can use the yellow zone to coach the two defenders regarding staying compact and covering the central area of the pitch. If an attacking player makes a run into the yellow zone, it may be to try to pull a defender away from the target area, and defenders should show disciple to stay central. If a player passes the ball to the attacking player in the yellow zone, the closest defender may go to press the ball; however, the central defender remains in the middle to help protect the target line or central area. If the defenders win the ball, they should aim to pass it to the next attackers in the line because it's important to always promote attacking transition when the defenders win the ball.

VARIATIONS

- Increase or decrease the area size to challenge or support players.

- Implement a rotation so all players can work on attacking and defending 2v2. Rotate the players so they can practice working with the yellow zones, both to their right and their left.

COMPONENT 2: 4V4 DEFENDING

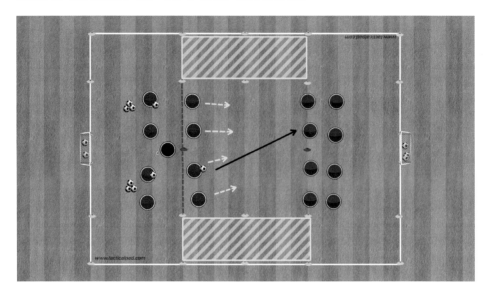

Figure 130. Similar to component 1, this progression creates a 4v4.

ENVIRONMENT

This exercise is a progression from component 1. Lift the central line of red cones and combine the players to create a 4v4 in the central channel. The red team passes to the blue team and plays 4v4 within the area. As with component 1, the team in possession can utilize the wider areas shown in yellow (see fig. 130); however, out-of-possession teams can enter those channels only when the ball does. The attackers aim to get across the dotted red line, whereas the defenders aim to stop the attackers from crossing the line, win the ball if they can, and look to pass to the next four attackers—simulating a forward pass after winning the ball.

BEHAVIORS

Encourage the attacking team to utilize the width and players to look to create length by moving higher up within the area. Also encourage them to cause the defenders problems by attempting penetrating passes, runs, and dribbles to get the ball across the red line while controlling the ball. In contrast, the defending team should look to stay compact and work as a unit to deny the attackers from progressing. If a player passes the ball into a wide area, the closest player may put pressure on the ball while their teammates supply cover centrally.

VARIATIONS

- Increase or decrease the area size to challenge or support players.

- You can provide an extra incentive for both teams by altering the setup so when players cross the red line they can go toward a goal and finish unopposed. You can implement this for the defenders also—if they win the ball, they can drive forward across an end zone before shooting on goal.

COMPONENT 3: CHANNEL GAME

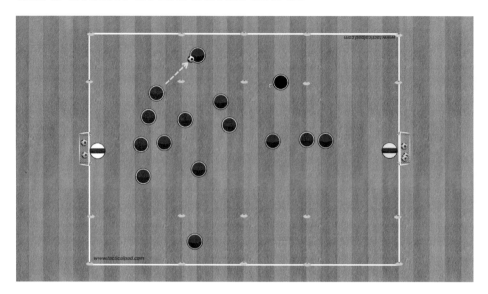

Figure 131. Play a normal game but with the wide channels in play for the attacking team.

ENVIRONMENT

By simply removing the final two red cones, the setup will now be ready for a game utilizing a wide channel on each side of the pitch. Simply play a game of soccer with the condition that players from the team in possession can use the wide channels at any time, but the team out of possession can enter the channels only when the ball is in there.

The use of wide channels encourages teams in possession to utilize as much space as possible in an attempt to draw the defending team away from the central area or goal they're protecting. The channels will encourage defending players to stay central and compact and press from an angle when a player receives the ball in a channel. All the while, their teammates should be supplying cover with no players in the channel at the opposite side of the pitch, as this would keep them too disjointed from their team.

VARIATIONS

- Increase or decrease the area size to challenge or support players.

- To further challenge the defending capabilities of each team, you can implement one or two playmakers to play for the team in possession.

- Play the game with the offside rule in play.

COMPONENT 4: PLAY A GAME

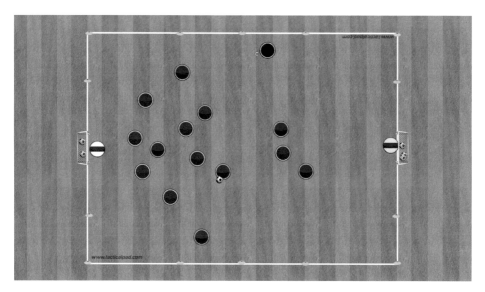

Figure 132. You can play a normal game with or without conditions that bring the focus of defending to the surface.

ENVIRONMENT

Progress to playing a normal game. You could implement a condition to bring the focus of defending to the surface, such as a team with a two-goal lead not being allowed to score a goal.

BEHAVIORS

This condition allows players to apply a defensive mindset when they go up 2–0, 3–1, or 4–2, for example. When they have the ball, they can work on keeping possession and managing the game to keep the ball away from their goal, and when they don't have it, they can transition to working on the defending behaviors practiced throughout the previous exercises.

VARIATIONS

- Increase or decrease the area size to challenge or support players.

- Play without conditions or instructions.

CURRICULUM: Strategy Soccer

SESSION: 3

AGE: 12+

STAGE: Learn Football

THEMES: Switching Play, Scanning, Composure, Range of Passing, Striker Movement, Progressive Possession

COMPONENT 1: PASSING WITH PACE

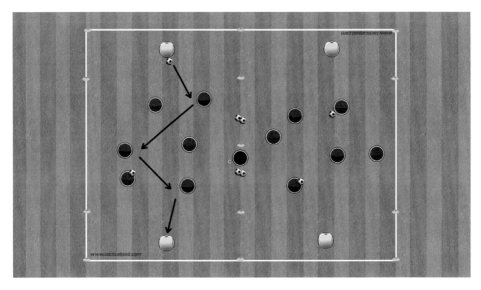

Figure 133. Players can use two playmakers to move the ball.

ENVIRONMENT

Each team has a ball, and this component focuses on circulating and switching the ball from side to side with as much pace and precision as possible. As figure 133 shows, the players in blue use each other and two white playmakers, who are situated on the outside of the area, to possess the ball. The red team does the same with their ball, using the two white playmakers. The exercise is split into two to maximize touches of the ball.

Players work on passing, moving, and supporting the ball constantly within this environment, all the while avoiding the obstacles created by the other team who's doing the same. Receiving the ball with an open body is likely to help with ball circulation within this exercise so players can assess where to pass the ball next. Encourage a variety of behaviors, such as bounce passes, driven passes, disguised passes, and give-and-gos within this environment.

VARIATIONS

- Increase or decrease the area size to challenge or support players.

- Minimize the number of touches each player can use, to further stress the importance of scanning and receiving with an open body position.

- Allow white-team players to play directly to each other, meaning central players can try to open up this pass before going to support the ball on arrival to the opposite white-team player.

- Facilitate a competition between the four active teams, giving a point for every time the ball is switched from wall player to wall player. The first team to do this six times wins.

- Frequently rotate the wall players.

COMPONENT 2: PASSING WITH PACE PROGRESSION

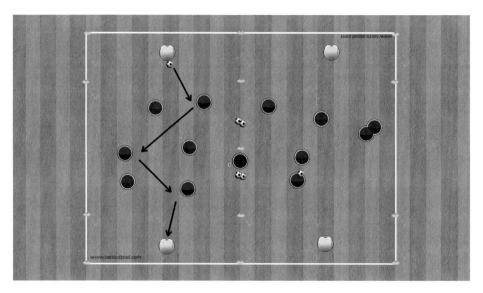

Figure 134. As a progression to Component 1, each team is now competing for the same ball and aim to keep possession of that ball using the Playmakers.

ENVIRONMENT

Teams play against each other 3v3+2, using wall players. The aim of this possession exercise is to transfer the ball from one wall player to the other. Teams may go back to the wall player they received the ball from, as patience to create the opportunity to switch the ball may play a crucial factor in not giving away possession.

BEHAVIORS

The three central players should be mindful and energetic in their approach to create passing options for the player on the ball. I often speak to the players I work with about giving options right, left, near, and far. Figure 134 shows an example of this: The wall player in white has the ball, and the blue team in possession is giving a variety of options. There's a player to the left of the ball who's near, looking for a pass. The player to the right has gone a bit farther, and the other player has moved away to create space and perhaps support to get the ball after the next pass. All three players have also tried to leave the passing lane open for the wall player to the other wall player, giving yet another option for the player on the ball. Players should try to recreate these options as the ball travels to other teammates, making it difficult for the defenders to cover and nullify all potential paths of the ball.

VARIATIONS

- Increase or decrease the area size, to challenge or support players.

- Minimize the number of touches each player can make, particularly for the wall players, as this will further challenge the support play of the central players.

- Initially, make it so central players can't tackle wall players, but you can progress the exercise to allow them to do so.

COMPONENT 3: PENETRATING PASSES

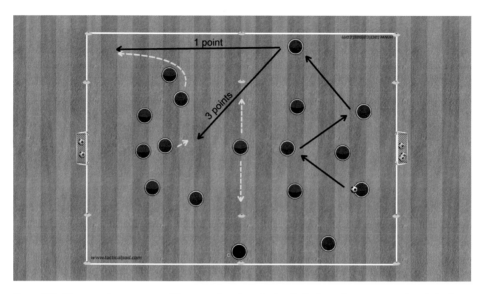

Figure 135. Players work as a group, with a screening player having limitations of movement and goals having a varied value.

ENVIRONMENT

The group works as a whole during this component. On one side of the area, the 5v3 from the previous component remains consistent, with five reds playing against three blues (see fig. 135). The aim of the five reds is to work the ball and create an opportunity to play forward into the other half of the area, where there will be a 3v4 to goal. The blue team has a screening player who can move only between the two central cones (see fig. 135), in an attempt to block forward passes centrally. If the red team plays a pass through these central cones and it results in a goal, the goal is worth three points. If the red team is unable to play through the central area and decides to play down the side of these cones instead, a resulting goal is worth one point. If any blue-team player wins the ball, they transition to try to score, and the game instantly becomes a free-flowing game, where players of both teams can move anywhere. Start the next ball with the blue team. The blue-team player who was screening the central gate can drop into the blue team's half to create 5v3, while a red-team player from their half becomes a screening player for this repetition. Essentially, the setup allows teams to take turns regarding switching the play to play forward, either centrally or via the wide areas.

BEHAVIORS

Players should demonstrate patience and the other behaviors honed during components 1 and 2 during the 5v3 buildup phase. Since the attacking players are 3v4, it's likely that players in the 5v3 will need to keep the ball for a period of time to find the opportune moment to play a player who can create a goal-scoring chance despite being outnumbered in the attacking half of the pitch. The front three have a chance to work on striker movement regarding dropping deep to receive a ball through the lines or making runs in the wide channels.

VARIATIONS

- Increase or decrease the area size to challenge or support players.

- Play with goalkeepers.

- Allow a player in the 5v3 to join the attack when the ball goes forward, creating a 4v4 to goal.

- Allow players in the 5v3 to dribble through the central gates or down the wide channels to join the attack.

COMPONENT 4: PATIENT BUILD UP

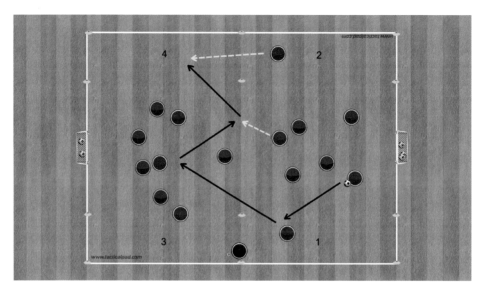

Figure 136. Moving the ball and therefore the opponents into wide areas will likely create opportunities for teams to score centrally.

ENVIRONMENT

Using the same setup as throughout the session, teams now play with completely free movement. You might implement a condition to bring the theme of switching play to the surface by highlighting to the players the four zones shown in figure 136—essentially where the wall players were standing in components 1 and 2. Condition the game so that before a player can score they must touch the ball in at least two of these zones, and the ball needs to travel via the central area before going into the next zone. Players can play the ball directly from zone to zone, but it counts as visiting two zones only when it goes via the central channel.

I find that this condition can be a great tool to demonstrate to the players how beneficial the behaviors of patience, switching the play, and circulating the ball can be to create opportunities to go forward and score. When switching from zone one to two (via the central zone, for example), it can help for players to draw the opposition into their half and give space for passes over or through the opposition and toward their goal. When switching from zone one to four (see fig. 136), this can pull the defenders of the other time into wide areas of the pitch and create space centrally for crosses or cutbacks that lead to goal-scoring opportunities.

VARIATIONS

- Increase or decrease the area size to challenge or support players.

- Further encourage buildup play by progressing the condition. Every zone visited is a point, and those points transfer to goals if the move is finished with a goal. I think this helps players recognize when there isn't a goal-scoring opportunity, and instead of forcing a shot, they can look to build up more points by, for example, going back to zone one, then switching to zone two and keeping the ball in areas of the pitch where they want to draw the opposition, and they therefore create a better opportunity to go forward and score.

- Play without conditions or instructions.

CURRICULUM: Strategy Soccer

SESSION: 4

AGE: 12+

STAGE: Learn Football

THEMES: Pressing as a Team, Recognizing Triggers to Press, Transition, Counterpressing, Creativity, Shooting

COMPONENT 1: PRESS THE BALL

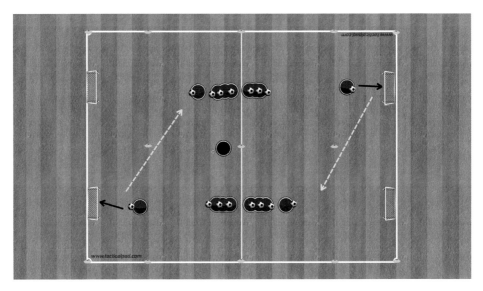

Figure 137. The blue player shoots, then turns to defend against the red player's shot.

ENVIRONMENT

Set up as shown in figure 137, with the final line of yellow cones indicating a shooting zone. The first blue player on each side drives into the shooting zone and shoots. Immediately after the blue player strikes the ball, the first red player attempts to drive into the shooting zone and is defended by the blue player who just shot. Players can score in either goal. Essentially, players attack, defend, and then join the other line in preparation for their next turn.

When attacking, players should look to drive with the ball using close control and a sharp and exaggerated change of direction to get past the defender before accelerating forward and finishing in the goal with power and accuracy. The defender works on quick reactions to shut down the attacker, looking to quickly deny the attacker of time and space. The attacker can't score until they enter the scoring zone. This gives the defender an opportunity to work on the angle at which they press the ball. A defender is likely to get more success if they press in a manner that blocks off a path to one of the goals. This narrows the attacker's options from going to either goal to having to travel toward the goal the defender is showing them toward. If the defender can successfully show the attacker to one goal, this will increase the defender's chances of making an interception or communicating to win the ball. Dictating the direction of travel for the attacker will certainly help the defender stifle the attacker's time and space on the ball.

VARIATIONS

- Increase or decrease the area size to challenge or support players.

- You may use goalkeepers in this exercise, which would take away the need for a scoring zone.

- Allow the defenders to score in one of the goals if they win the ball.

- Between the two lines of attackers, add an extra goal the defenders can transition to when winning the ball.

- Set a time limit for the attacker to score, to encourage quick play in 1v1 attacking situations and also to work on the defender's ability to delay and slow down attacks.

COMPONENT 2: COMMUNICATE AND PRESS

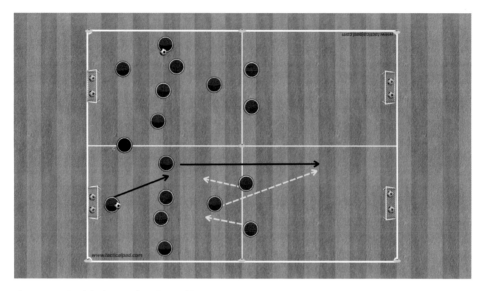

Figure 138. The defenders on the other half (shown in red) can press once they think they have a chance to win the ball. Once those defenders move in, only then can the team in possession move to the other half and attempt to shoot on goal.

ENVIRONMENT

The team in possession plays in a 4v2 rondo, attempting to keep the ball. They must constantly be scanning and aware of incoming defenders. The two defenders on the other half can come and press the ball whenever they think there's an opportunity to win the ball. Only once the extra defenders enter the rondo (creating a 4v4) can the team in possession (in fig. 138, the blue team) look to break out of the half and toward the goal.

BEHAVIORS

The two defenders waiting to press should look to identify a trigger to press, giving themselves the best possible opportunity to win the ball. A trigger may be an under-hit pass, a poor touch, or perhaps the angle at which their teammates press the ball. When not pressing, they should be shifting side to side in relation to the ball. The team in possession should be working on circulating the ball and waiting for an opportunity to play forward. Once their passing has enticed the extra defenders (they may intentionally hit a soft pass to draw them in), they can then look to make forward dribbles, passes, and runs to advance toward the goal. At that point, the game becomes a 4v4 until a player scores a goal or the ball goes out of play.

VARIATIONS

- Increase or decrease the area size to challenge or support players.

- Utilize a bonus-ball system once the exercise becomes a 4v4 game.

COMPONENT 3: HIGH PRESS

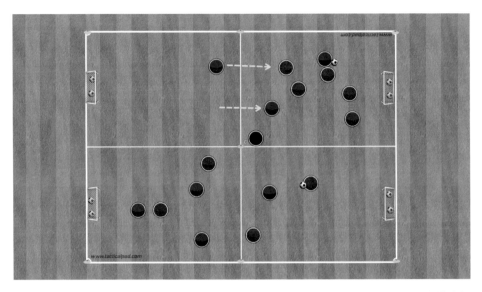

Figure 139. Players run a 4v4 game with the condition that the entire team must be on the attacking half of the pitch for a goal to count.

ENVIRONMENT

Run 4v4 games on each side of the pitch with an obvious halfway line present in both games. To encourage pressing and counterpressing, introduce the following simple condition to this game: for a goal to count, all players of the team must be beyond the halfway line (in the attacking half).

BEHAVIORS

Working as a unit is crucial to get success in this game. Teams must sit in their own halves, staying compact and disciplined, looking for an opportunity to pressure and win the ball. When this happens, they must quickly transition forward with the entire team moving together. This eases the pressure from their own goal but also keeps heat around the ball should they lose possession in the opposition's half. They'll have players close enough to counterpress and try to win it back if they move up the pitch with the ball. Encourage, coach, and discuss triggers to press and ways to help one another win the ball. On the flip side of this, the players in possession are provided with a great environment to work on playing out of a high-pressure press and being able to keep the ball in crowded areas. This small-sided game should allow for a lot of individual technical development.

VARIATIONS

- Increase or decrease the area size to challenge or support players.

- Rotate the teams after each game—for example, the red teams can swap pitches.

- Play a competition. For example, every team plays each other once—three points for a win, one for a draw, and zero for a loss.

COMPONENT 4: PRESS AS A TEAM

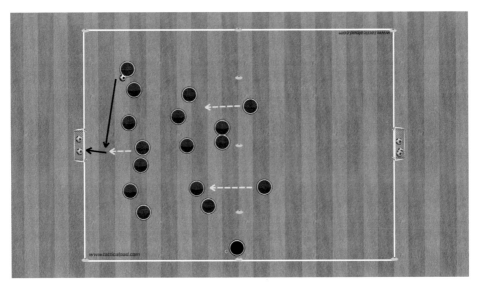

Figure 140. Combine the players to create two teams playing in a larger area. Again, a goal counts only if the entire team is past the halfway line.

ENVIRONMENT

This is a simple progression from component 3, combining the players to create two teams playing in a larger area. Teams play a game, again with the simple condition that a goal counts only if all players from that team are past the halfway line (yellow cones in fig. 140).

BEHAVIORS

Providing players with plenty of game time allows them to work on all the behaviors encompassed within a game of soccer, such as passing, dribbling, teamwork, defending, attacking, and transition. But this simple condition will put extra emphasis on what's been worked on throughout the session—putting pressure on the ball, pressing, and counterpressing as a team, then transitioning toward goal.

VARIATIONS

- Increase or decrease the area size to challenge or support players.

- Implement the offside rule.

- Use goalkeepers if possible.

- Reward positive play by stipulating that if a team scores, they restart with the ball.

- Play without conditions or instructions.

CURRICULUM: Strategy Soccer

SESSION: 5

AGE: 12+

STAGE: Learn Football

THEMES: Shooting, Rebounds, Defending, Decision-Making, Combination Play

COMPONENT 1: COMBINATION TO SHOOT

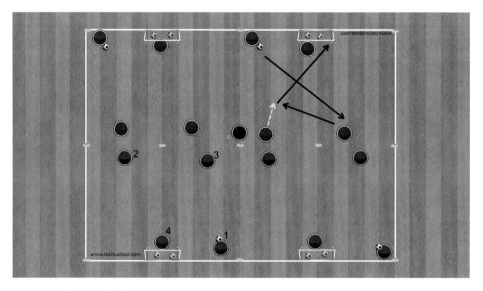

Figure 141. Players work in four stations, and this rotation is replicated four times.

ENVIRONMENT

This shooting exercise is replicated four times (see fig. 141) to maximize repetitions for the players. The balls start at player one. This player passes to player two, who lays the ball off for player three, who shoots on player four. All players then rotate around one position (after the shot has been taken to ensure safety): number one becomes number two, two becomes three, three becomes four, and four becomes number one. They pass, lay off, shoot, save, get a ball, and go again. After a certain number of repetitions, be sure to start the ball at the other side of the goal also, to work on shooting from a different angle.

BEHAVIORS

The player at station one should touch the ball and look to hit a driven pass with power and accuracy on the ground to player two. Striking through the ball and in the middle will help, as will aiming a pass with the big toe of the player's standing foot. They should avoid hitting underneath the ball as this will lift the ball off the ground and make it harder to control. The player at station two should look to take some of the power off the initial pass by gently laying it off in front of player three, who will step on and strike the ball. This environment allows for maximum repetition, meaning players can learn through trial and error the striking technique that works for them, but as the coach, you may need to give some pointers regarding striking through the ball, aiming for the corners, and applying disguise to shots in order to elude the goalkeeper.

VARIATIONS

- Increase or decrease the area size to challenge or support players.

- Implement competition between the four players, seeing who can score the most goals.

- Implement competition between the four groups shown, seeing which group can score ten goals first (you may want to supply a goalkeeper from an opposition team).

- The player at station two could vary the feed (a gentle hand throw, for example) so players can work on volleys and half volleys.

- After passing, the player at station one could become the defender to create a 2v1 to goal.

COMPONENT 2: SHOOTING AND REBOUNDING

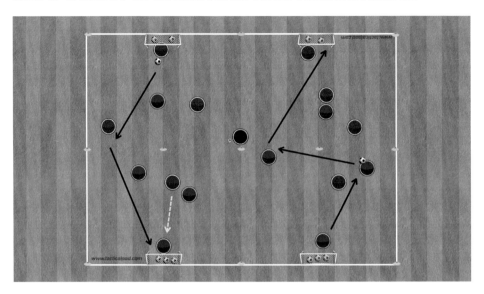

Figure 142. Players must stay on their half of the pitch for the entire game. Each team has three players on one half and one on the other.

ENVIRONMENT

Play two games of 4v4 but adjust the numbers of players and pitches as needed. Here, each team has three players in one half of the pitch and one in the other, and players must stay within their halves for the duration of the game. Use an area size that allows players to work on shooting from the zone where they have the 3v1 overload. As shown in the diagram, players use their 3v1 scenario to try to create a chance to shoot from their own half. Again, the pitch should be small enough that shooting from a player's own half is a realistic shooting distance.

BEHAVIORS

When in possession in a 3v1, players try to create an opportunity to shoot, avoiding the player who's pressing but also avoiding the players in the other half who are likely trying to block the attacker's shot. Reward players who strike the ball with power and pace by stipulating that when a player scores a goal the team who scored restarts with possession of the ball (have balls in each goal to allow for quick restarts). The player isolated in a 1v3 situation should attempt to press the ball and shoot if they win it. This player should also work on their rebounds, working hard to make reacting to a teammate's shot a habit they take into games. I've seen some excellent creativity come to the surface within this environment, with players shaping up to shoot from their half, then cleverly playing a disguised pass to the player in the other half, giving them an easy finish.

VARIATIONS

- Increase or decrease the area size to challenge or support players.

- As figure 142 shows, a player in the team of three can become the goalkeeper when their team doesn't have the ball, or you could introduce goalkeepers to the exercise.

COMPONENT 3: SCORE THEN SAVE

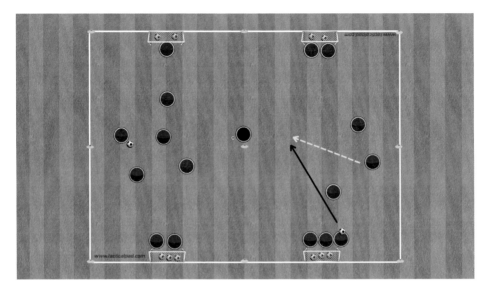

Figure 143. Once a player scores, they stand in the goal and become a goalkeeper. The first team to get all their players in the goal wins.

ENVIRONMENT

Removing the halfway line from component 2, play small-sided games, still utilizing small pitches to allow for shooting opportunities regardless of where players have the ball. The game starts with no goalkeepers. For example, the layout shown in figure 143 would be 4v4 on the pitch with no goalkeepers. When a player scores a goal, they stand in the goal and become a goalkeeper. The next player to score for their team joins them in goal, as does every goal scorer after that. The first team to have all their players in the goal wins.

BEHAVIORS

An array of behaviors will come to the surface within this environment. It's a fun and intense game that creates 2v3s, 1v1s, 4v2s, and more. Shooting, rebounding, and creating space via foot skills and dribbling are all crucial behaviors practiced within this environment. Once a team has one or multiple goalkeepers, they can use them as wall players. This gives players a great opportunity to pass the ball back to the goalkeepers, then work on movements and runs to receive the ball in goal-scoring positions (see fig. 143).

VARIATIONS

- Increase or decrease the area size to challenge or support players.

- Be mindful of the age and stage of your players and use these shooting exercises only with players who can carry them out safely.

- If you're running two, three, four, or more pitches with this exercise, you can implement a league-table idea, playing each game for a set amount of time, with the winning team moving up a league and the losing team moving down. The winning team is the one with the most goals when the time runs out.

COMPONENT 4: AREA OVERLOADS

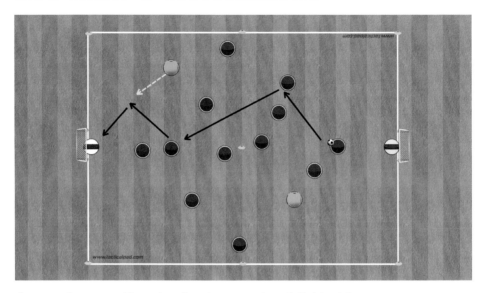

Figure 144. Play a 7v7+2 with two playmakers who must stay in one half of the pitch.

ENVIRONMENT

This environment involves a game of soccer; however, a playmaker plays for the team in possession in each half of the pitch. This creates overloads to help bring to the surface the themes of creating chances, shooting, and rebounding. Numbers can be flexible, but figure 144 shows a 7v7+2 game. The playmakers must each stay in one-half of the pitch.

The extra player will help not only in the attacking half when it comes to creating opportunities to shoot but also in the team's own half when the team has the ball there, since there's an extra player to help the team find forward passes and supply their attacking players with the ball. This environment will likely give you an opportunity to coach a variety of forward passes and support play from teammates when the ball does go forward. The overloads created can help coaches demonstrate to players the value of disguise—looking to pass but then shooting or looking to shoot but then playing a disguised pass to a teammate so they can shoot.

VARIATIONS

- Increase or decrease the area size to challenge or support players.

- You might have specific players you want to utilize as playmakers—those who play as more attacking players or maybe those who need to work on shooting and attacking play.

- Play without conditions or instructions.

CONCLUDING THOUGHTS

Thank you for taking the time to read this book. I hope the Scoreboard Soccer concept is something you can apply within your coaching practice. I hope your players find the scoreboard games as fun as the players I work with find them and that they benefit from all the hidden learning created within the Scoreboard Soccer environment.

If I had to leave the reader with one parting thought, it would be this:

This book was written in 2021. If the content is delivered to a group of ten-year-olds, they'll likely still be playing the game in 2040. Who are we to know what the game will look like in the future! Give your players the space to play and to have fun. Promote positive behaviors, such as confidence, dribbling, communication, and teamwork, and above all, inspire creativity and welcome problem solving. These are the players to show us what the game could look like in 2040. These are the people who will evolve the game.

APPENDIX

Table 2. Suggested Playing Area Dimensions

PLAYERS	DIMENSION (YARDS)
11v11	110 × 70
10v10	90 × 60
9v9	80 × 50
8v8	70 × 50
7v7	60 × 45
6v6	55 × 40
5v5	45 × 35
4v4	40 × 25
3v3	30 × 20
2v2	25 × 15
1v1	15 × 12